CREATE

IN ME A

CLEAN

HEART

RAY BEESON

THOMAS NELSON PUBLISHERS
Nashville • Atlanta • London • Vancouver

Published in Nashville, Tennessee, by Thomas Nelson, Inc., Publishers, and distributed in Canada by Word Communications, Ltd., Richmond, British Columbia, and in the United Kingdom by Word (UK), Ltd., Milton Keynes, England.

Unless otherwise noted, Scripture quotations are from the NEW KING JAMES VERSION of the Bible. Copyright © 1979, 1980, 1982, Thomas Nelson, Inc., Publishers.

Scripture quotations noted NIV are taken from the HOLY BIBLE, NEW INTERNATIONAL VERSION ®. Copyright © 1973, 1978, 1984 by International Bible Society. Used by permission of Zondervan Bible Publishing House. All rights reserved.

The "NIV" and "New International Version" trademarks are registered in the United States Patent and Trademark Office by International Bible Society. Use of either trademark requires the permission of International Bible Society.

All italicized portions of Scripture passages that appear in this book are the author's.

Library of Congress Cataloging-in-Publication Data

Beeson, Ray.
    Create in me a clean heart : prayer and Scripture to cleanse and make whole / Ray Beeson.
        p.   cm.
    Includes bibliographical references.
    ISBN 0-7852-8081-2
    1. Holiness—Christianity. I. Title.
BT767.B44   1995
248.3—dc20   94-34369
                                                           CIP

Printed in the United States of America
1 2 3 4 5 6 7 - 01 00 99 98 97 96 95

To Rob
A wise son makes a glad father.
Thank you.

Contents

$\mathcal{A}$CKNOWLEDGMENTS

I am so grateful for the assistance of Judith Hayes, whose writing and editing skills were invaluable to this project. Her insights into many spiritual truths are profound.

Thanks to Pastor Dave Guzik, who has taken an interest in my writing over the years. He is truly a man of encouragement.

Writing a book can be a long and difficult process. A good publishing editor like Lonnie Hull DuPont ensures that the end result will be rewarding. She is truly a professional whose goal is excellence.

Thanks to my wife, Linda, who has stood beside me faithfully for more than twenty-five years. Her sweet and gentle spirit continues to enrich my life.

$\mathcal{I}$NTRODUCTION

Living the life of a consecrated Christian and being "faithful" are not always easy. I doubt they have been for anyone. A close walk with God often includes injustices from without and sorrows from within. There is also the pain that comes from simply feeling inadequate as a Christian.

My own struggles in Christianity have not been primarily with overt sin or with repeatedly falling to temptation. My greatest struggle is a dilemma that has been much more subtle. It has to do with little things—a small failure here, a frailty there. I strive to walk in the Spirit, and yet I find that I'm not nearly the spiritual person I'd like to be. Sometimes it seems that the harder I try, the worse things seem to get. I find myself looking introspectively at my own heart, perhaps as David did in the Psalms. I'm ever so aware of God's great holiness and my own insufficiency.

Much to my relief, God has heard my heart's

cry and has given me confidence and direction. I attribute some of my growth and development to two cherished prayers prayed by King David and recorded in Psalm 51:10: "Create in me a clean heart" and "Renew a steadfast spirit within me." I'm astonished at how these simple prayers have been so life-changing. I'm grateful for their effects, and I am confident that they will work similarly for you.

It all began quite casually. These prayers became a deep, inner cry within my heart, similar to what David must have experienced. Slowly I sensed something happening. More of the fruit of the Spirit—love, joy, peace—seemed to be developing within me. Many of my disagreeable and unpolished mannerisms began to be replaced with more gentle and sensitive attitudes. There is no doubt that much of this process could also be attributed to the maturity that develops as a natural part of Christian growth. But I believe in my heart that much of this growth would have been delayed and perhaps would not have happened if I had not prayed those prayers.

Over a period of time, I have added eighteen more life-changing, spiritually cleansing prayers to this list. These prayers continue to minister to me each time I pray them, and they have stimulated my ongoing spiritual growth and intimacy with God.

Each chapter of this book is about one of those one-line, powerful prayers. As you read this book, you may want to pray these prayers daily for a while, concentrating on various aspects of each one as it affects your own life. Tremendous healing and restoration will take place as you spend time with your heavenly Father, developing with him both closeness and confidence.

I have included a personal prayer at the end of each chapter to guide you as you pray. My hope is that you will find these prayers particularly helpful during times of crisis, times when oppression and fear come to destroy your peace, times when you are about to embark on a new spiritual journey, or times when you simply want to refresh yourself and draw nearer to God.

If you are rather new to the experience of prayer, I invite you to join me and discover the beauty of prayer and the peace that it brings. It requires some patience. Prayer is a little like a transfusion: some prayers work only a drop at a time, but in the end they prove effective, and things change. I believe that your life will be touched and transformed as you pray. May you prosper and be blessed from reading and praying these prayers.

Ray Beeson

CHAPTER 1

CREATE

IN ME A CLEAN

HEART

Let my heart be blameless regarding Your statutes, / That I may not be ashamed.

(Ps. 119:80)

"Then I will give them one heart, and I will put a new spirit within them, and take the stony heart out of their flesh, and give them a heart of flesh, that they may walk in My statutes and keep My judgments and do them."

(Ezek. 11:19–20)

A number of ducks became ill with a contagious and deadly disease that threatened the lives of other healthy ducks. The California State Game Department ordered the birds destroyed. Words of outrage came immediately from irate bird lovers, demanding a halt to the plan. There was contention on both sides of the issue. Too bad the ducks couldn't have voiced an opinion. If they had had the slightest bit of humanness in them, we might have heard something like this: "There's nothing wrong with me any more than any other duck in this pond"; "I'm no worse than anyone else I know of around here"; "Sure, maybe I'm a little sick, but we've all got to die someday."

We are like those sick ducks. We can't see it, but our deplorable condition is drastically affecting others. We are sick. However, in *our* case the sickness is not limited to our physical bodies. It's in our souls, or as King David said, our hearts. After only a casual look at our world, it becomes readily apparent that something is wrong someplace inside each of us.

The difficulty, to one degree or another, has to

do in part with our wills, minds, and emotions. There is something flawed in our ability to decide and choose, to think and reason, and to sense and feel. Fortunately for us, there is a cure. But often we try to buy healing from spiritual pharmacies that dispense worthless, man-made medicines. Or we fail to find the cure because we believe that it must come from within our own strength and ability—and we've already learned that we can't accomplish much by ourselves.

God's solution to our problems begins when we invite him into our lives. He wants to work deep inside us to initiate change. "For it is God who works in you both to will and to do for His good pleasure" (Phil. 2:13). The apostle Paul's message was "Christ in you, the hope of glory" (Col. 1:27).

Jesus spent a great deal of time bringing help, hope, and comfort to his disciples. Then he spoke of leaving them. What a letdown that must have been at the time! But Jesus was sensitive to their needs, assuring them that they would not be left comfortless. They were not to worry when he was gone because he was going to send them a Comforter—one who would walk alongside them to give the same counsel and assistance that he had been giving. But the amazing thing about this new order was that this Comforter, who is the Holy Spirit, would not only walk alongside them; he would actually be *in* them (John 14:17).

God's workings by his Spirit deep within the human spirit, however, are usually not well understood. Most of us don't readily perceive what it is that he wants us do. His intentions are often lost in a sea of confusion and disagreement over petty and insignificant religious issues that have nothing to do with what he is trying to accomplish in us—one of which is character development. God's desire is that all of the base and defiled things in our lives, all negativism, bitterness, and hatred, be removed and be replaced with the love of God. He wants to change us into what he originally intended us to be.

Spiritual cataracts on the eyes of our understanding, however, prevent us from seeing that God has freely offered to personally work in us and to make changes in us that we cannot make on our own. God will literally work by his Spirit inside a person who will grant him permission to do so. "If anyone is in Christ, he is a new creation" (2 Cor. 5:17). And that is precisely what the gospel message is all about—becoming *new inside.* It is not being made better; it's being made *new,* and Christ is the agent for that change. Radical, drastic, and wonderful transformation is God's order for the person who will freely submit to him.

But we are afraid of change—afraid that God will do something to us that we don't want done. Make no mistake; God will not force anyone into anything. He is not interested in controlling humanity. He wants humanity in control of itself. That, however, happens only through a relationship with Jesus Christ.

Worthless legalisms that have been handed down from previous generations scare many people away from a commitment to Christ. We Christians are often the ones who most discourage others from coming to Christ. Unhealthy lifestyles, the justification of sin, narrowmindedness over issues that have nothing to do with salvation and with eternity, and ethics and morality that are no different from that of the world are all things that cause people to reject Christ. If God "causes" such weirdness in people, then who in their right minds would be interested in letting him work in them?

Christians, as well as non-Christians, are afraid of change for other reasons also. The religious tirade that demands submission to God's full control and insists that true dedication is not achieved without a complete passive obedience (no wants and desires of our own) is wrong and dangerous. If God were interested in passive submission, it would be his on demand. One word from him would bring all of humanity to its knees. Manipulation and domination are not in the mind of God. He is interested in a personal and loving relationship with us, one in which our wills continually come into line with his will through his loving persuasion.

God knocks at the door of the human heart with offers of newness, restoration, and healing. Unfortunately, many people continue to deny him entrance and, as with the sick ducks, something eventually must be done.

By the time we reach adulthood, most of us realize that we have internal problems. Depression, discouragement, worry, anxiety, and fear are warning signs that all is not well. The problem is in our hearts, which God enters only after receiving our permission. When God gave us free will, he intended to preserve it. Free will is vitally important to a creature who was intended to have within him God's image and likeness, and God won't arbitrarily violate that free will. In other words, God won't do anything in us contrary to our will.

If God were to hinder our ability to choose, he would severely hinder our character and personality development. Choice is important in order to escape the realm of robots. Choice prevents a person from becoming machinelike. The problem is that freedom of choice means that we must be allowed to choose other than what is good and healthy for us. We must be allowed to choose not to love as well as to love. Real choice means that I can even become my own god and worship the creature rather than the Creator. Our world is a picture of people who have done exactly that.

For humanity to be rescued from its own rebellion, the only solution is for the heart to be changed through willing cooperation. Until then there is no hope for any kind of permanent restoration and wholeness. For this reason, Jesus stands humbly at our heart's door, requesting entrance. His advance is just that—a request. God literally asks for our permission and cooperation in order to make us what he originally created us to be. Once we consent to do God's will, he makes us able to accomplish it.

We picture Jesus as a lamb, not only because

he was the substitutional sacrifice provided for our salvation, but because of the tenderness with which he approaches the human heart. Notice the gentleness in his words in Revelation 3:20: "Behold, I stand at the door and knock." There is compassion even as we are bid to come work in his kingdom. "Come to Me, all you who labor and are heavy laden, and I will give you rest. Take My yoke upon you and learn from Me, for I am gentle and lowly in heart, and you will find rest for your souls" (Matt. 11:28–29). The day is coming when the Lamb will descend again to earth, but this time as a lion—the Lion of the tribe of Judah. The tenderness will turn to judgment as the Lion proceeds to put this planet back into proper order.

In the meantime, God's plan for inner restoration continues. He is looking for those who will freely submit to him. And he will not introduce change within us unless he has our full and willing cooperation. He is ready to do the work when "you search for Me with all your heart" (Jer. 29:13).

King David apparently understood this plan. He saw himself as God saw him, and recognized that in his defiled condition there was no hope for abundant life without a new heart created within him: "Create in me a clean heart," he cried (Ps.

51:10). God's willingness to do the work blended with David's willingness and hunger to have the work done.

In God's plan for human restoration, the heart (including the will, the mind, and the emotions) begins to experience change upon conversion. Old ideas and old ways of thinking begin to pass away while new ideas and new ways of thinking begin to develop. That change continues for a lifetime. Along with that process is a need for periodic cleansing from the sin that sometimes is allowed back into our lives. Christ, our advocate, stands ready to help us whenever necessary: "If we confess our sins, He is faithful and just to forgive us our sins and to cleanse us from all unrighteousness" (1 John 1:9).

When given permission, the Spirit of Christ cleanses the human heart of desires and actions that are damaging to itself and to others. It would be good if we could pray for cleansing just one time and experience a change so radical and lasting that there never again would be a need for another request. That is not the case. The change that God effects is a process—one that is continuous and gradual. At each juncture in the road toward wholeness, he asks our permission to continue.

And there are times when he says nothing and does nothing, but instead waits for us to ask him for help. Sometimes he waits until our desire literally becomes a passion. It is not until we cry out like David, "Create in me a clean heart," that our hungering and thirsting for righteousness allows God to remove our rebellion, like removing rust from the stuck hinges of the many closet doors deep within our hearts.

Let's consider four things that are necessary for the development of a clean heart. First, we must recognize that we have a problem. Who can submit to change without understanding that something is wrong? Restoration and reconstruction are not possible without a damage assessment. The "If we confess our sins" of 1 John 1:9 suggests that we are aware of our condition. As we become ready and able to listen, God begins to point to things that need to change—thoughts, attitudes, habits, what we eat and drink, and much more.

Second, we must be willing to be changed. We must be convinced that God is not out to harm us. We must believe that only good will come from whatever he intends to do. Sometimes it is easy to believe that God will manipulate us into something other than what we want to be, that he will destroy something in us that we consider to be sacred.

Third, we must admit that we cannot change ourselves. Sometimes God has to allow us to struggle and fail while we try to find perfection in the power of our own flesh. When we finally discover that all such striving is in vain, we become ready for the work that only he can accomplish in us.

The fourth step is to *ask* God for help. To finally come to a place of saying, "Lord, I need you" is to come to where he can begin to make us whole.

Father God,
I really do need you. Something deep inside me
cries for what I believe only you can satisfy. I
need to be clean from within. Wash me and
cleanse me. Make me the person you originally in-
tended me to be. Show me the changes that need
to take place, but more importantly, give me the
means to accomplish them.

CHAPTER 2

*R*enew a

Right Spirit

within Me

. . . Renew a *steadfast spirit* within me.

(Ps. 51:10)

"I will cleanse you from all your filthiness and from all your idols. I will give you a new heart and *put a new spirit within you*. . . . I will put My Spirit within you and cause you to walk in My statutes, and you will keep My judgments and do them."

(Ezek. 36:25–27)

*N*othing in life is more difficult to control than those two tameless beasts, the tongue and the emotions. Someone cuts us off in traffic, and our tempers flare. Caustic words come our way and we feel we must respond in kind. We must equal or surpass the offensive actions in order to even the score. We mark off territory like the neighborhood cat, and pounce on anyone foolish enough to violate our space.

All of us face the temptation to act inappropriately in many situations. Things come our way that move our emotions radically, pushing us out of control. We tend to react by saying and doing things before we think. The problem is that we are dominated by our emotions. This is tragic for a Christian because out-of-control emotions tend to override the fruit of the Spirit. Love, joy, peace, kindness—all of them suffer at the hands of a fiery, excitable soul whose hysteria is not easily checked.

The more we mature in our experiences with God, the more powerful we become in spirit and the less we are dominated by inappropriate emotional reactions. God's desire is to produce in the human spirit the beauty, wholeness, and power that it had in Adam before he rebelled. Perhaps God intends to give us more in Christ than was lost in Adam—that the redeemed man or woman is ultimately greater than the innocent Adam. To receive such redemption, our spirits must become more powerful than our soulish emotions. And in order for that to happen, our spirits must be made right.

The key to the development of a right spirit is intimacy with God. King David prayed for God to renew his spirit. David wanted his words and actions backed up by clean and guileless motives and attitudes. He knew that the deepest part of his being, his spirit—the breath and true essence of his person—also needed to be restored to its original intended condition and purpose.

God is willing to work deep within our spirits to help make changes *if* we are willing for the work to be done. He will literally change attitudes if allowed to do so, and changed attitudes mean different behavior and different lives. But the work will never take place until we express a desire for it in prayer.

Unfortunately, some Christians place most of their emphasis on outward conduct rather than on inward attitudes, and nothing within them changes very much. They've got the process backward. The outside of the cup appears clean, but the inside remains filthy and full of greed, selfishness, and self-deception. Exterior holiness creates haughtiness and pride, and falsely separates people with these attitudes of superiority.

Right actions, although they are necessary, may not always reveal the true attitudes and motives going on inside. We can be persuaded to do almost anything, and in the process be little more than play actors. We tend to convey one thing on the outside, while something else is going on internally. We are like the disobedient little boy who was told to sit in the corner. "I may be sitting down on the outside," he said, "but I'm standing up on the inside."

The spirit of a person largely determines who he or she is. Negative, bitter, and critical attitudes reflect a spirit that is not right with God. These attitudes conspire to create dissension, disunity, backbiting, gossip, and a host of other evils that work at destroying the individual and others around him or her. God wants these attitudes changed and the resulting evil actions stopped. Nothing is more important to him than refocusing our blurred spiritual vision and developing a right spirit within us.

God made us for himself. He created us in his image and likeness in order to have fellowship and union with us. He wanted us to have a caring and a loving relationship with him and with other people. But Adam's rebellion changed the godly image and likeness originally given to him. He no longer resembled God. We now bear Adam's likeness—one that is full of anger, hatred, bitterness, and other destructive characteristics—and we continue to pass these evils on to our offspring.

If two people are to walk together in harmony, they must be alike in spirit. The same is true with God and his people. Our spirits must be like his Spirit if we are to be close to him. If we want to know what his Spirit is like, we must look at his nature. His nature is revealed in his names—Counselor, Comforter, Prince of Peace, Shepherd, Father—the list is extensive. Each name gives insight into his character and tells us what God is really like.

Of all the words and names that describe God, perhaps none is more appropriate than the word *love*. Whatever this word truly means, it is what God is. And it is what our nature is to be like as well. This is clearly spelled out in any agreement that God ever makes with humanity. God bases his relationship with an individual on two commandments: Love the Lord your God and love your neighbor as yourself (Matt. 22:37–40).

God's nature is love. If we want to walk with him in oneness, our nature must possess the same characteristics as does his. A right spirit, then, is a loving spirit, one that is concerned about God and about others. It is full of joy, peace, patience, kindness, goodness, faithfulness, gentleness, and self-control. That means that it is cleansed of hatred, discord, jealousy, fits of rage, selfish ambition, dissensions, factions, and envy (Gal. 5:20–21). It is understandable, then, that walking with God is a process. Our relationship with him grows deeper as changes transpire.

This does not mean that we have to be perfect before we can really experience God. It means that the intensity of the relationship grows as we are being changed into his image. And our growth depends on our prayer.

A true believer may occasionally fall into sin but does not make a practice of sinning (1 John 3:6, 9). Negative attitudes will always be around to influence the Christian life. Part of the battle we face is making sure that they do not attach themselves to our lives.

Without a right spirit, attitudes that include negativism, bitterness, and criticism become the forces behind our actions. These attitudes soon invite fear, worry, anxiety, depression, and discouragement to join them, producing powerful influences that affect ourselves and others in injurious ways.

It isn't only what a person does that affects others for either good or bad; it is also the way in which the person does it. Two people give a speech. One person is loud, crude, and pompous, while the other is quiet, humble, and reserved. Words and actions may be similar, but the outcome is drastically different because of the different spirits within these two people.

Two other people try to influence a situation. One succeeds while the other fails. In the end, both have said basically the same thing. The only difference was the spirit in which it was said.

The spirit of a person is like a fragrance. Some people add a sweetness and pleasantness to their surroundings, while others produce an aroma like that of a threatened, defensive skunk.

The condition of a person's spirit determines,

to a large degree, how much he or she will be either accepted or rejected by others. Even positive actions may be rejected because of the person's destructive attitudes.

The peacefulness or agitation of a person's spirit is sensed more than it is seen. Even without many words or facial expressions or much body language, we often communicate in spirit that we are happy or sad, encouraged or discouraged, or that we have embraced any one of a host of other attitudes. And *attitude* generally describes the kind of spirit that a person possesses. Temperaments that consistently display hatred, jealousy, and vindictiveness toward others carry within them elements of evil. A true salvation experience begins with the Holy Spirit moving to change these and other wrong attitudes. Salvation takes hold by more than just being sorry for our sins. It begins by covenanting with God to reverence him and to be concerned about others. In fact, all of the books of the Law and Prophets can be summed up in those two commandments concerning love (Matt. 22:40).

The Spirit of God cannot fellowship with a person who says, "I can forgive, but I cannot forget." Certainly the memory of past wrongs will haunt the soul, trying to flood and fill the mind. Satan's demons know how to attack our thought lives. That is why we are to cast down improper imaginations and thoughts (2 Cor. 10:3–5). But when we make the statement about forgiving but not being able to forget, perhaps we haven't done any real forgiving; we haven't allowed the love of God to penetrate our hearts and spirits. Sometimes the very tone in which we speak reveals the negative spirit still residing within us.

Certainly, we must realize that the deeper the pain, the more difficult it is to deal with forgiveness. And sometimes the process takes a long time. The important thing is to let the Lord take us on a journey of restoration and to ask for his help even when we feel like giving up.

A right spirit does not become right on its own. No amount of time will bring it to a place of love while it is having problems with hatred and self-centeredness. That is why David backed up his decision for change by crying out to God for help.

Dear God,
I recognize that my attitudes toward you and to-

ward others are sometimes negative. I confess this. Place a new spirit within me, one that is fashioned after your own Spirit.

CHAPTER 3

*G*RANT

ME TRUE

HOLINESS

Hear my prayer, O LORD, / And let my cry come to You. / Do not hide Your face from me in the day of my trouble; / Incline Your ear to me; / In the day that I call, answer me speedily. / For my days are consumed like smoke, / *And my bones are burned like a hearth. / My heart is stricken and withered like grass, / So that I forget to eat my bread. / Because of the sound of my groaning / My bones cling to my skin.*

(Ps. 102:1–5)

"For I will restore health to you / And heal you
of your wounds," says the LORD.

(Jer. 30:17)

*S*ome churches discourage
their people, and especially
their youth, from participating in fun activities in
which non-Christians may be present. Movies,
roller skating, and bowling are sometimes on this
list. Understandably, they want their young people to be holy. They reason that Christians who
are set apart from the world will more likely reach
the goal of holiness. How Christians can work in
the same places, eat in the same restaurants, and
shop in the same stores alongside unbelievers and
still maintain their holiness is somewhat of a mys-
tery in relation to this theology. These necessary
things in life are usually allowed, but recreation
can be enjoyed only with other believers—other
believers, that is, who believe the same way as this
particular group.

Certainly Christians need to be different from
unbelievers. But the approach to being "set apart"
must be biblical or it can be as destructive as

outright worldliness. Many people have become casualties to a misdirected emphasis on holiness and righteousness. They have lost their commitment to Christ over a standard that was faulty—a standard they could not live up to.

Motives in churches like these may be good, but the result is often a misunderstanding of what it means to be holy. Holiness to some people is wrapped up in a person's ability to perform correctly. What one does or does not do constitutes holiness. Although there is a small amount of truth in this reasoning, the greater amount of error eventually destroys lives. The problem is an inability to comprehend true holiness.

To understand holiness requires first a recognition of the difference between holiness and righteousness. Holiness is a state of being. It is intrinsic value and perfection. Something is either holy or it is not. If it is not complete, or whole, then it is incomplete or fragmented, and not holy.

Righteousness, however, is the *result* of holiness. In other words, a whole person does right things. If my hand is broken, no matter how hard I try to immediately make it work right, it won't work because it isn't whole. But once it becomes whole it will work just fine.

If we confuse holiness and righteousness, or misdefine them, we end up with a form of godliness void of any goodness or power. Think of holiness as *wholeness*. Holiness, or the lack of it, can be described by the condition of our entire being—body, soul, and spirit. And we must be whole wherever wholeness is possible if we are to effectively practice righteousness.

One of the reasons why God doesn't arbitrarily condemn us is that we are unable to make ourselves whole in order to practice righteousness. We are no more capable of restoring our damaged condition than we are of adding two inches to our stature. Our responsibility before God is to allow him, as the Great Physician, to fix what is wrong.

It is no secret that humanity has some terrible problems—that our world is not whole. No matter what we do on our own to make ourselves more complete, we never accomplish the goal. Something in our lives always remains fractured and incomplete. If God does not step in to help, we are without hope. God's desire is to restore us to holiness (wholeness), to make us complete once again.

It is true that righteousness contributes to holiness, especially when we consider the condition of our bodies. More accurately, righteousness *maintains* holiness. Good food, proper rest, and sufficient exercise all add to a wholesome body. But no matter how well we treat our bodies, we can never restore them to perfect wholeness. At best, we slow down the deterioration process. Only in the resurrection will our bodies be completely restored. However, our souls and spirits are currently in the process of being restored.

The salvation message not only means an escape from eternal separation from God, but it also suggests the restoration of every part of our being. Whereas we are entirely saved when we come to Christ, we might look at three distinct aspects of restoration. First, our spirits *are* restored to God at conversion. They are set apart for God when we bow our knees to Jesus. Humbling ourselves before him brings a change in our spirits. Second, our souls, especially our minds and our emotions, are in the process of being set aside for God's glory. We might say that our souls *are being* restored. Third, our bodies have yet to put on immortality. Eventually we will have new and transformed bodies, so we say that our bodies *will be* restored. Someday they will be whole again.

We refer to God in terms of holiness because,

unlike us, he is flawless. He is perfect and complete in every aspect. His holiness gives us perspective and insight into our own condition by comparison. God is the blueprint. How could we really evaluate our condition if a pattern didn't exist? Jesus turns out to be the actual pattern. It is through him that God reveals his fullness to humanity. "For it pleased the Father that in Him all the fullness should dwell" (Col. 1:19). "For in Him dwells all the fullness of the Godhead bodily" (Col. 2:9).

Holiness is not a standard that God maintains. It is not something he does. It is who and what he is. God doesn't proclaim his holiness in order to oppressively lord it over humanity. He shows us who he is in order to model what we are to be like.

But we cannot be restored to that condition without God's help. No amount of personal righteousness will achieve holiness. Nothing we can do, other than to grant God permission to work within us, will ever make us whole. This is why our prayer is not "*teach* us true holiness," but rather "*grant* us true holiness." It is a plea to have something done in us that we cannot do ourselves.

This is not to say that righteousness is unimportant. It is to say that holiness and righteousness must not be confused if we are to experience and taste both. Holiness begins with the restoration of a person's spirit to God. Righteousness begins when actions are correct. The more aligned our spirits become with God's Spirit, the more righteousness will flow out of our actions.

Here is why self-righteousness is so destructive. When we act self-righteously, we give the appearance that all is well between ourselves and God when in reality nothing has happened in our spirits. Self-righteousness gives the devil the opportunity to suggest a backward theology: that good deeds make a person fit for heaven.

When we ask God for a right spirit, we are asking him to begin in us the process of developing holiness. When we ask for a clean heart, we are asking for his help in developing right actions.

We refer not only to God as holy but to his Word as holy as well. Solomon said, "Every word of God is pure" (Prov. 30:5). God's words are flawless because he is flawless. Therefore, we use his word as a mirror to determine our own holiness/wholeness.

God's Word is the divine representation of who he is. "In the beginning was the Word, and the Word was with God, and the Word was God" (John 1:1). God's Word and his character are the same. That is why we call it the *living* Word. "And the Word became flesh and dwelt among us" (John 1:14).

The more we have of the Word of God in us, the more we have of his character, nature, and Spirit, and the less we are found in sin. King David said, "Your word [the character and nature of God] I have hidden in my heart / That I might not sin against You" (Ps. 119:11). Not only did David know the Scriptures; he also knew the character of God in his heart. God testified, "I have found David the son of Jesse, a man after My own heart, who will do all My will" (Acts 13:22).

The apostle Paul understood these truths and expressed them in his words "that I may know Him" (Phil. 3:10). Paul wasn't looking for an introduction; he already knew Jesus. He wasn't seeking salvation; he had been assured of that earlier. What he wanted was to have in himself everything that was in Jesus. He spoke of the Spirit of God dwelling in the believer. He encouraged the Philippian Christians to let the mind of Christ be in them (Phil. 2:5). Paul never stopped desiring, pursuing, and preaching that the very character and nature of God could be imparted to us through Jesus.

Grant Me True Holiness   **29**

Father God,
From your Word I now know that my body, soul,
and spirit have been damaged because of sin. Re-
store me and make me whole. I give you permis-
sion to work in me, to reconstruct every fiber of my
being, that I might reflect your image and like-
ness.

$\mathscr{T}$EACH

ME TRUE

RIGHTEOUSNESS

Open to me the gates of righteousness; / I will go through them, / And I will praise the LORD.
(Ps. 118:19)

I will instruct you and teach you in the way you should go; / I will guide you with My eye.
(Ps. 32:8)

$\mathscr{S}$omeone asks the question, "If salvation is by faith, then why do I have to be good?"

Another person believes that God's grace is so

great that we can do virtually anything we want, even if it's wrong, and God will forgive us.

The first person is confused, but the second person is deceived. One is trying to understand truths that seem to be in opposition. The other has carelessly accepted a theology without considering the whole counsel of God.

We must not minimize God's great grace in emphasizing our need for right living. In other words, we don't want to be so legalistic that we live apart from God's willingness to forgive us of our sins. At the same time, we don't want to dishonor him by allowing his grace to become a license to sin.

Both of these people need to understand that although we can never be good enough to merit our own salvation, right living does more than simply glorify God: it also prevents the enemy of our souls from finding points of entry into our lives. Sin destroys life as well as allows Satan's army of deceiving spirits to further invade our lives to affect others negatively.

For some people the concept of righteousness suggests a very dull and unexciting way of life. They believe that righteousness and enjoyment cannot coexist. This distortion of God's intention for His people is a deception of Satan. It is one of Satan's lies that is designed to rob believers of joy, refreshment, and a deep sense of God's grace in their personal lives.

The devil would love us to believe that God is a joyless individual who discourages happiness. "After all," Satan points out, "look at the sadness and misery in the world around you. If God wanted people to be happy, he would do something about all the suffering and sorrow." Some Christians have been so affected by this lie that they have come to believe that the more spiritual a person is, the more that person will appear somber and downcast.

Satan lies to us continually by saying, "God doesn't want you to sin because he doesn't want you to have fun." Satan creates a mentality that says, "Righteousness is too restrictive. It is not possible to live with any degree of happiness and fulfillment by doing what God says is right."

The truth is that God doesn't want us to sin because sin doesn't work. God didn't create us to do the things he forbids; we were not created to accommodate sin in our lives. Countless victims of sin bear witness of this by their shattered and broken lives. Adultery is wrong and counterproductive because it destroys relationships, leaving spouses and children emotionally scarred for life. Lying, cheating, and stealing are immoral and unethical because they directly hurt other people. Toying with anything that God forbids in his Word and trying to make it work will always bring disappointment. Sin, by definition, is missing the mark. Eventually it becomes unsatisfying, self-defeating, and just plain destructive. We cannot mock God and his guidelines and hope to be blessed and vindicated.

Scripture speaks of putting on righteousness both as a shield and as a garment (Eph. 6:14, Ps. 132:9). In the book of Revelation, fine linen at the wedding of the Lamb represents the righteous acts of the saints (Rev. 19:8). We are to be clothed in that fine linen every day.

Salvation does not come from doing good deeds; rather, good deeds come from being saved. "For by grace you have been saved through faith, and that not of yourselves; it is the gift of God, not of works, lest anyone should boast" (Eph. 2:8–9). Note also Romans 3:19–20: "Now we know that whatever the law says, it says to those who are under the law, that every mouth may be stopped, and all the world may become guilty before God.

Therefore by the deeds of the law no flesh will be justified in His sight, for by the law is the knowledge of sin."

Jesus taught that righteousness drew humankind to the Father: "Let your light so shine before men, that they may see your good works and glorify your Father in heaven" (Matt. 5:16). Paul's teaching reflected the need to live according to God's standard: "But you have not so learned Christ, if indeed you have heard Him and have been taught by Him, as the truth is in Jesus: that you put off, concerning your former conduct, the old man which grows corrupt according to the deceitful lusts, and be renewed in the spirit of your mind, and that you put on the new man which was created according to God, in true righteousness and holiness" (Eph. 4:20–24).

Good deeds cannot produce salvation; again they are to be an outgrowth of it. James wrote:

> *What does it profit, my brethren, if someone says he has faith but does not have works? Can faith save him? If a brother or sister is naked and destitute of daily food, and one of you says to them, "Depart in peace, be warmed and filled," but you*

*do not give them the things which are needed for
the body, what does it profit? Thus also faith by
itself, if it does not have works, is dead. But someone will say, "You have faith, and I have works."
Show me your faith without your works, and I
will show you my faith by my works.* (James 2:14–
18)

Righteousness also protects us from Satan's
influence in our lives. Adam was free from satanic
bondage and control until he sinned. Our whole
world is in the disastrous state that it is, not
because God delights in our pain, but because the
human race refuses to follow God and his commandments.

Righteousness is one of the defensive and pro-
tective pieces of armor provided by God for Christian battle. "Stand therefore, having girded your
waist with truth, having put on the breastplate of
righteousness" (Eph. 6:14). It's true that our primary protection comes from the righteousness
which is in Christ. "But of Him [God] you are in
Christ Jesus, who became for us wisdom from
God—and righteousness and sanctification and
redemption" (1 Cor. 1:30). But notice that his act

of righteousness was to produce righteousness in us: "[Christ] Himself bore our sins in His own body on the tree, that we, having died to sins, might live for righteousness" (1 Pet. 2:24).

Those who live righteously are less likely to become casualties in this spiritual battle. King David knew that and prayed to that effect: "Let integrity and uprightness preserve me, / For I wait for You" (Ps. 25:21).

Our righteousness protects other people as well. "For you, brethren, have been called to liberty; only do not use liberty as an opportunity for the flesh, but through love serve one another. For all the law is fulfilled in one word, even in this: 'You shall love your neighbor as yourself.' But if you bite and devour one another, beware lest you be consumed by one another!" (Gal. 5:13–15).

Since the fall of Adam, humanity has often questioned God's commandments and intentions. We test God, try God, and even challenge God; but in the end we all come face to face with our finality and God's divinity. If we insist on sowing to the flesh, we must reap the unpleasant consequences and learn that God is holy and unchangeably righteous.

Righteousness is also the development of a

clean heart. It is God's masterpiece: the maturing of our wills, minds, and emotions. Making wise choices, thinking pure thoughts, and expressing appropriate emotions are all evidences of redemption and righteousness at work. Ethical and moral purity and awareness of right and wrong are the signs of a person who is advancing in righteousness. But such growth and change can never occur in the power of our own strength. That is self-righteousness, and it looks favorable only on the surface. It is not the evidence of good character development.

Christianity is never quite so exhausting and discouraging as it is when we try to live it by personal effort. The harder we try to be righteous and good, the worse we often become. The more we want to do for God, the less we often accomplish. God never stands back demanding that we strive to do or to be something in our own strength. It is foolish and dangerous to think that the commandments of God are to be fulfilled without his help. "For we are God's fellow workers; you are God's field, you are God's building" (1 Cor. 3:9).

Dear Lord,
I desire to know you and your ways. I long to rest
my head upon your chest and hear your heart-
beat. Father, teach me how to trust you and rely
on you in a brand new way. Teach me to discern
my self-efforts from your holiness, righteousness,
and grace. I surrender my heart to you. Show me
how to glorify your name, especially in right liv-
ing.

CHAPTER 5

*H*ELP ME

TO BE OBEDIENT

TO YOUR WILL

Show me Your ways, O LORD; / Teach me Your paths. / Lead me in Your truth and teach me, / For You are the God of my salvation; / On You I wait all the day.

(Ps. 25:4–5)

The steps of a good man are ordered by the LORD, / And He delights in his way. / Though he fall, he shall not be utterly cast down; / *For the LORD upholds him* with His hand.

(Ps. 37:23–24)

*I*s it possible to want to love and serve God and at the same time intensely dislike the idea of obedience? For those whose concepts of submission and compliance suggest bondage, it *is* possible. No word seems more difficult to deal with than the word *obey*—especially for those whose obedience has been forced.

Obedience describes a relationship between two parties in which the one in authority commands while the other submits. We struggle with this relationship for two reasons. First, we wrestle with the rebellious nature with which we were born. Each of us came into this world with an instinct of self-preservation that focuses on our own needs before those of anyone else. Our own wants and desires become so demanding that we develop a "Don't get in my way, and don't tell me what to do" attitude. Some of us are inclined toward self-will more than others, but that basic self-centered nature still exists in all of us.

Second, we have a feeble understanding of what obedience really is. The hypocritical attitude that says "Do as I say, not as I do," and the domineering attitude that demands complete

Help Me to Be Obedient to Your Will **41**

compliance or else, both work to distort the true nature of authority and of God's pure intentions. Our need for obedience does not arise out of one of God's needs. God has no need to feel in control.

The design of obedience was never meant to bring bondage into anyone's life. On the contrary, the whole idea of authority was meant to protect and to preserve the human race. Our own self-centeredness and our painful experiences at the hands of others have helped to pervert a beautiful and vital part of our relationships.

We can think of dozens of questions about how and when we are to submit to authority. We can also deliberate about why we shouldn't obey at all. But there is really very little validity in these kinds of discussions until we become convinced that submission is indeed legitimate in and of itself. Many people believe in obedience but are motivated only by fear. Some of them drive the speed limit simply because they are afraid of getting a ticket. Many people obey their bosses only to keep from being fired. Even God is reverenced by some people only because of the fear of hell and eternal damnation. It is possible to obey in actions and still not submit in heart.

We respond with real obedience when we recognize God's right and obligation to speak into our lives—a right that he will not exercise without our permission. God speaks in two primary areas. First, he makes general statements to all of us through his written Word. What he says to one person equally applies to all. Second, he speaks to each of us in specific ways about our personal lives. To everyone he says, "Love one another," and gives us other instructions that safeguard the human race. To individuals he gives various personal directives. To one he may say specifically, "Love Jim." To another he says, "Go to this place and help." And to still another he says, "Change your attitude."

Christians who are only casually committed to God usually find themselves struggling with the fundamental elements of God's will as revealed in his Word. Those who are deeply committed usually wrestle with the need for direction in their personal lives with questions such as, "Lord, what is my ministry? How can I use my gifts to serve you better? How can I be more pleasing to you?" They have no question as to the need to obey God's written Word and known will. What they want to find is his perfect will in personal directives that are not spelled out in detail in Scripture.

The apostle Paul would refer to the first group

of believers as carnal. They still live in bondage to sin. The second group may not be in bondage to sin, but their lives are not without difficulties either. If Satan can't prevent us from serving God, he will try to drive us too far in the opposite direction. Consequently, some dedicated believers develop an inordinate fear of missing God's will. They live under constant pressure, striving to obey and please God with a lingering fear of eventual failure. God has become their taskmaster. But as with any tactic that the enemy of our souls tries to use to destroy the believer, God works to make that difficulty a blessing if we continue in faith—that is, if we are tenacious in our desire to be whole as well as to be obedient. If we keep going, God will eventually deliver us from misconceived concepts concerning his nature.

Performance that is generated by fear always ends in exhaustion. Even with a healthy approach to Christian living, the many little do's and don'ts of our experiences tend to wear us down after a while.

God allows each of his children to strive in the flesh as a Christian, because he knows that each of us will come to a place where we hit a dead end. This is a necessary experience for developing spiritual growth. Not until we have exhausted every ounce of our own strength in serving the Lord and are worn out mentally, physically, and spiritually do we find a hiding place in God called *grace*. That place—grace—is free from worry, fear, anxiety, confusion, and especially the guilt associated with obedience that never seems to make the grade. Not until we become convinced that all of our self-efforts, no matter how hard we try, will always fall short of the Law, do we find the grace of God. Then we discover a new walk by faith, not by performance. Only when we are out of breath spiritually and can't find the strength to take another step are we ready to experience a new understanding of our relationship with God, one in which our heavenly Father becomes our "Daddy." Jesus taught this greater intimacy with the use of the word *Abba,* a word thought by some to convey a deeper, more personal meaning in the relationship.

Often this deepening experience makes us aware for the first time that God is not our task-master or our strict disciplinarian, but our loving, concerned Father in heaven.

Father God,
Thank you for expressing your love and concern
for me. It makes it much easier for me to yield my
life to you. But, Father, I still need your help in
doing the things that please you. For the most
part, I believe I want to do what is right, but
every time I turn around I'm tempted to do wrong.
I need your strength in order to overcome the
many things that try to draw me into sin.

CHAPTER 6

SAVE SOULS

AND TOUCH LIVES

THROUGH ME

*Oh, do not let the oppressed return ashamed! /
Let the poor and needy praise Your name.*

(Ps. 74:21)

"Is this not the fast that I have chosen: / *To
loose the bonds* of wickedness, / To *undo the
heavy burdens*, / To *let the oppressed go free*, /
And that you *break every yoke*? / Is it not *to
share your bread* with the hungry, / And *that
you bring to your house the poor who are cast out*;
/ When you see the naked, *that you cover him,*
/ And not hide yourself from your own flesh?

/ Then your light shall break forth like the morning, / Your healing shall spring forth speedily, / And your righteousness shall go before you; / The glory of the LORD shall be your rear guard. / Then you shall call, and the LORD will answer; / You shall cry, and He will say, 'Here I am.'"

(Isa. 58:6–9)

*P*erhaps no transition in life is as wonderful and dynamic as that of going from self-centeredness to caring for others. That's difficult for some of us. Bars on the prison of self keep us from reaching out to touch each other. To move from self-centeredness to deepening relationships of love and concern for others is to move the soul from incarceration within itself to wonderful freedoms of fellowship with both God and other people. When we are still in bondage to ourselves, we possess a deception that keeps us from experiencing one of the greatest joys of life—the joy of investing personally in someone else.

Once we have been freed to love, we find it difficult to understand how we ever could have been deceived into believing that promoting good in the life of another would only detract from ourselves. We have become free to care and to love, and free from the worry, anxiety, depression, and discouragement that characterize a person overly concerned with self.

Some professional people understand this freedom in bits and pieces and will tell us that few things are more fulfilling in life than their experiences with helping others. The physician who has just completed a successful operation, the firefighter who rescues a child from a burning building, and the police officer who prevents a mugging all know the thrill of doing something for someone else. Even the person who looks like every other face in the crowd and yet takes the time to hold the door for someone frail knows briefly that there is something right about doing good.

But care and concern for others doesn't come easy, especially when our own physical, mental, and emotional needs are so demanding. It takes a giant leap of faith to believe that if we turn away from personal concerns to help someone else, even for a moment, our own needs will still be met.

Sometimes it's hard to believe that other people are worth loving. When hatred and bitterness stand in the way, we have more than just our own needs blocking the road to finding the joy of loving others. Even though the hatred may seem justified because of abuse suffered at the hands of another person, the result is the same: hatred destroys relationships, and relationships are the foundation of life.

God never meant for us to live any other way than in a corporate setting. The idea that no one is an island is a biblical truth. We were not made to live by ourselves or within ourselves. "Confess your trespasses to one another, and pray for one another, that you may be healed" (James 5:16). "Be completely humble and gentle; be patient, bearing with one another in love" (Eph. 4:2 NIV).

We may find, at times, that our own prayers do not get answered until someone else begins to pray for us. Likewise, some of their prayers may not be answered until we join with them in prayer. It's possible that God may not answer individual prayers as much as he does corporate prayers to show us that we need each other. This prevents us from turning toward pride or self-centeredness. If we came to a point of not needing anyone else, we would violate God's plan for fellowship and be stripped of some of the safeguards that prevent

Satan from deceiving us. The body of Christ is made up of many members, none of whom can operate completely alone. We need each other. "The body is one and has many members, but all the members of that one body, being many, are one body" (1 Cor. 12:12). "Again I say to you that if two of you agree on earth concerning anything that they ask, it will be done for them by My Father in heaven" (Matt. 18:19).

If we have trouble getting our prayers answered, we should try a new approach. We must take time out first to genuinely pray for others. "And the LORD restored Job's losses when he prayed for his friends. Indeed the LORD gave Job twice as much as he had before" (Job 42:10). Next, we need to incorporate other people into our prayer requests. We need for them to pray *with* us as well as *for* us.

Our concern for the physical and emotional well-being of another person is admirable, but going a step further and being concerned about his or her eternal soul is greater still. We must not become self-centered either as groups or as individuals and fail to see the need to reach out to those who are unsaved. When we tenderly and patiently confront unbelievers with the gospel in a loving manner, they begin to realize that we really do care about their souls. "And he who wins souls is wise" (Prov. 11:30).

Dear Lord,
I do not want to be selfish and self-centered. My
desire is to love you and to love others. Place in
me your concern for those around me, and help me
to reach out to them with love and a helping hand.

$\mathcal{K}$EEP ME FROM

EVER BECOMING

A WICKED PERSON

Direct my steps by Your word, / And *let no iniquity have dominion over me.*

(Ps. 119:133)

"I will make an everlasting covenant with them, that I will not turn away from doing them good; *but I will put My fear in their hearts so that they will not depart from me.*"

(Jer. 32:40)

$\mathcal{T}$he closer we get to God and the deeper our relationship grows with him, the more readily we see how really deficient some of our attitudes and actions are. We must reconsider our old notions of "I do the best I can" and "I don't hurt other people" when we begin to understand that what we believed to be the smallest of sins hurts someone else. Sin is missing the mark, and the "mark" is to love God and to love others.

It is important to understand that God isn't condemning us when he points to our problems. He does not identify our sins in order to dishearten us or wound us, but to restore us to wholeness so that we can enjoy the good things in life. When God says that a certain thing is wrong, it is because somewhere in the actions or attitude behind it there lies something damaging to ourselves or to others. Often, in examining our own behavior, we fail to look deeply enough into our hearts to really see what it is that we are doing that might be hurting ourselves or others.

Until it dawns on us that all our righteousness is still no better than filthy rags (Isa. 64:6), we may be tempted to gloat over our own self-righteousness. Every man, woman, and child on the face of the earth was conceived and born into a state of sin (Ps. 51:5) and then raised in a world "under the sway of the wicked one" (1 John 5:19). In order for us to live right, the effects of sin and Satan must be removed from our lives.

The influence of evil is dismantled progressively as we enter into a deeper relationship with God. Step by step, God leads and guides the person once programmed by sin into a new life of holy living in him. We need to understand both the desired outcome and the process.

God is interested in restoring our innermost being; that is the desired *outcome*. His goal is to develop within us character and personality that produce love for him and for others. It is easy to get sidetracked from the process of inner development by any number of things. Legalistic religion can get in the way. Traditionalisms that have nothing to do with real righteousness can be a problem. Some people get caught up in political religion and miss the beauty of the transformation process.

The *process* that God allows for inner development is important for us to understand as well. As much as we may not like it, God uses suffering and sorrow to develop depth of character in his people. He may not create our trials, but he certainly allows them in order to mature us. "We also glory in tribulations, knowing that tribulation produces perseverance; and perseverance, character; and character, hope" (Rom. 5:3–4). What happens *to* us is not nearly as important as what happens *in* us from God's perspective.

We are people in process. From the first day that we allow him access to our lives, he is at work within us. That means that inwardly we are to be changing, maturing, and growing. If we question whether or not we are progressing well, we must evaluate whether or not we are growing in greater degrees of love and unity within the body of Christ. If we hold unforgiveness, bitterness, envy, criticism, and hatred toward others, our religion is in vain. If we believe that our church is the only true church, we have become deceived, and the love of God is not in us. We must never forget that God loves the whole world. His concern for the restoration of people does not evaporate when he sees our frailty, our disposition toward sin, or even our failures. God is faithful to keep pursuing us and to keep on working for us simply because he loves us.

Maturity is a sign that the salvation we received from Jesus is working. "Giving all diligence, add to your faith virtue, to virtue knowledge, to knowledge self-control, to self-control perseverance, to perseverance godliness, to godliness brotherly kindness, and to brotherly kindness love" (2 Peter 1:5–7). Stop and ponder each of the above; they are important.

Most of us can look back along the road to maturity and recognize that the bumps and potholes we faced have deepened our understanding of life and have given us insight for the days ahead. What often we were not prepared for was the possibility of a collision that would leave our lives in terrible disarray. Who could foresee that there would be times in which parts of our lives would come to a screeching halt, only to be swallowed up in darkness and despair? Who among us can understand the loneliness of being stranded in the wreckage of an existence that once seemed so well centered in the fast lane of life?

A marriage falls apart, a child gets into serious trouble, or some other disaster strikes, and suddenly our world falls apart. The abruptness of such changes in life leaves many of us unable to continue on. Our hearts and emotions reel from the death of a family member or other loved one. We are often shocked at the loss of what appeared to be a secure place of employment. We are disappointed and hurt deeply when we are betrayed by an intimate friend or confidant.

Coping with these difficult situations, we can become disillusioned, unbelieving, and discouraged. It is precisely at this point that some of us are greatly tempted to turn back on our journey with God. The road appears too narrow and impossible to maneuver. God appears to have failed to give adequate warning signs for impending danger. And worst of all, God doesn't appear to be anywhere in sight amid the despair and darkness.

If you have been to this point in life, you are not alone. The children of Israel traveled this road and wanted to return to Egypt. Some of the disciples of Jesus became discouraged and no longer followed him. In reality, all of us sooner or later come to a crossroad where we are tempted to turn and walk away from him. If we find ourselves at this crossroad, it is essential that we keep going. God's greatest servants have been to this point in life. But what made them truly great was that they didn't turn back.

After being abandoned by a number of disciples, Jesus turned to those followers still remaining and asked, "Do you also want to go away?" Their heartfelt response was, "Lord, to whom shall we go?" (John 6:67–68). Our hearts' cry and deepest desire should be to *remain*—to pray for the courage to continue on God's pathway, to seek to live godly, moral lives, to fellowship with God, and to bravely abide with Christ in his sufferings. As we truly pray for answers and direction, our foremost question too will be, "Lord, to whom shall we go?"

> *Dear Lord,*
> *I desire to have a right heart—a clean heart*
> *washed and whole. I desire to honor you not only*
> *by my actions but by my attitudes as well. I know*
> *you can see into the hearts of all men and women.*
> *As you find any remnant of corruption in me, I*
> *ask that you touch me and make me whole and*
> *holy.*

CHAPTER 8

*F*ILL ME

WITH YOUR

HOLY SPIRIT

Do not cast me away from Your presence, /
And do not take Your Holy Spirit from me. /
Restore to me the joy of Your salvation, / And
uphold me by Your generous Spirit.

(Ps. 51:11–12)

"I will pour out My Spirit on all flesh; / Your
sons and your daughters shall prophesy, /
Your old men shall dream dreams, / Your
young men shall see visions. / And also on

My menservants and on My maidservants /
I will pour out My Spirit in those days."

(Joel 2:28–29)

*W*hat does it mean to be Spirit-
filled? The mark of a Spirit-
filled man or woman is the love, joy, peace,
patience, kindness, goodness, and faithfulness expressed toward others. Spirit-filled Christians are
those who are filled with the attributes of God.
They are concerned about other people, and they
want to walk worthy of God's calling "with all
lowliness and gentleness, with longsuffering, bearing with one another in love, endeavoring to keep
the unity of the Spirit in the bond of peace" (Eph.
4:2–3). The seal upon a Spirit-filled life does not
display itself in some unusual gift that sets believers apart, but in the fruit of the Spirit, which binds
us together. "Behold, how good and how pleasant
it is for brethren to dwell together in unity!" (Ps.
133:1).

The moment we begin to believe that we are
in any way superior to any other individual in the
body of Christ, we are deceived and gravely mis-

taken. Certainly God appoints people to various positions, offices, and callings that set them apart, but in God's sight we are all his sons and daughters, members of his royal family. There are no superstars in the body of Christ. The cost of my salvation and yours was the same as it was for everyone else.

If God works powerfully in us by his Spirit, what do we have to boast of? Were not the wonderful benefits all from God's enabling and empowerment? Didn't God choose us before we chose him? Didn't God love us before we learned to love him?

We learn to rejoice as God touches our spirits with his Spirit. To be filled with the Spirit means literally to be imbued, influenced, or supplied to the maximum. God's desire is to influence our spirits and bring them up to their full potential. That is his plan when he fills us with his Spirit.

All he needs is our cooperation in order to carry out his plan. God's Spirit will work within the human spirit only by permission. God is a gentleperson and will never impose his will upon anyone. When we open the door to him and invite him into our lives, he begins to replace the works of the flesh with the fruit of the Spirit (Gal. 5:19–23).

Create in Me a Clean Heart

Attitude is critical in the proper development of the human spirit. What we say is often less important than the way we say it. If Satan can manipulate our attitudes, he can eventually draw us into negativisms and destructive criticisms. These elements of ruin soon yield the additional poisons of bitterness and hatred, which damage human spirits as certainly as arsenic damages the human body. Division, arrogance, and spiritual pride then quickly spread to other soldiers in God's army, disarming them through discouragement and leaving them open and vulnerable to satanic attack.

The infilling of the Spirit of God is not a one-time experience; it is something that must happen progressively and continuously. Just as food and rest are necessary for the development and sustenance of the human body, so also the human spirit must regularly receive the ministry of the Holy Spirit in order to develop and to gain its highest potential. Another human spirit can do only so much to influence our spirits. Beyond that, we need God's sovereign touch. Only he can influence and ignite our spirits to bring us to complete fulfillment and fruition.

Left to itself, the human spirit soon succumbs

to the troubles and difficulties of life. "A merry heart makes a cheerful countenance, / But by sorrow of the heart the spirit is broken" (Prov. 15:13). "A merry heart does good, like medicine, / But a broken spirit dries the bones" (Prov. 17:22).

There are a number of ways in which the Spirit of God fills us. One of the most exciting and refreshing ways is when God does so in a sovereign manner. The human spirit simply and profoundly experiences the Spirit of God. The early church first experienced this on the day of Pentecost. God supernaturally visited them, and as a result, they were changed individuals.

God's Word, both written and spoken to our hearts, along with prayer and fellowship are three other ways that God influences our spirits. The Bible, unlike any other book, is a God-breathed book. Its inspiration develops spiritual life. When we read it, it changes our lives. Prayer is communication and fellowship with God. If we spend enough time with anybody, even in a purely social situation, they have an influence on us. When we spend time with God, his influence is profound. Fellowshipping with God's people promotes opportunities to love and to share, to support and to be supported, and to let iron sharpen iron. We also learn more about ourselves when we are with other people. The end result is spiritual growth.

If Satan despises anything, it is these three ways in which our spirits are strengthened. If we struggle with any one or all three of these ways, is it any wonder? The enemy will do everything possible to stop spiritual growth in a believer. Satan is threatened and intimidated every time we advance even a little in spiritual maturity and biblical principles.

It makes no sense to pray "Lord, fill me with your Holy Spirit" and at the same time be unwilling to cultivate and promote that infilling with the additional spiritual strength that comes from reading God's Word, spending time in prayer, and fellowshipping with other believers in the body of Christ.

The strongest soldiers in God's army have always recognized their need to depend on the mercy and truth that they have received from God's Spirit. David noted in the Psalms the protection and refreshing to his spirit that came from spending time alone with God. "But You, O LORD, are a shield for me, / My glory and the One who lifts up my head" (Ps. 3:3). God deeply desires to be the lifter of *our* heads.

Many a saint will testify that there is nothing more wonderful in all the world and nothing more satisfying to the human spirit than the renewal and restoration that comes from spending time in sweet fellowship with their loving Abba Father.

Dear Lord,
I know there is no abundant life in me outside the influence of your Holy Spirit. I desire to find your mercy and truth and to be refreshed and renewed by your Spirit. Teach me to wait upon you and for you. Please ignite my spirit, and fill and fulfill me.

CHAPTER 9

TEACH ME

TO DISCERN

GOOD FROM EVIL

I am Your servant; / *Give me understanding, /
That I may know Your testimonies.*

(Ps. 119:125)

*"Call to Me, and I will answer you, and show you
great and mighty things,* which you do not
know."

(Jer. 33:3)

*E*yesight is a wonderful blessing. To behold the delicate
beauty of a flower, to enjoy the unique colors of a

rainbow, to be touched by the smile of a baby are all miracles indeed. The ability to see never means quite so much to a person until it is lost and creation is hidden behind the veil of darkness. But physical blindness is not the only kind of "seeing" handicap we face: humankind experiences spiritual blindness as well.

Jesus spoke of men whose *hearts* were blinded:

Seeing they do not see, and hearing they do not hear, nor do they understand. And in them the prophecy of Isaiah is fulfilled, which says: / "Hearing you will hear and shall not understand, / And seeing you will see and not perceive; / For the hearts of this people have grown dull. / Their ears are hard of hearing, / And their eyes they have closed, / Lest they should see with their eyes and hear with their ears, / Lest they should understand with their hearts and turn, / So that I should heal them" (Matt. 13:13–15).

What a sorrowful indictment to be resting upon any human being!

Our world is filled with people who are without vision. They are unable to see and perceive spiritual matters properly. Therefore, they cannot see the myriad things around them, beginning with the God whose face shines in his creation. "For since the creation of the world His invisible attributes are clearly seen, being understood by the things that are made, even His eternal power and Godhead, so that they are without excuse" (Rom. 1:20). Jesus taught that such blindness was due to the fact that they loved darkness rather than light because their deeds were evil (John 3:19).

Even those who loved Jesus and walked with him possessed degrees of blindness. The disciples failed to make connections between matters in the natural realm and matters in the spiritual realm. Jesus warned them about the Pharisees, whose preoccupation with outward holiness and appearance had nothing to do with true righteousness. Jesus rebuked his disciples by saying, "Do you not yet perceive nor understand? Is your heart still hardened? Having eyes, do you not see? And having ears, do you not hear?" (Mark 8:17–18).

That kind of blindness still exists in the body of Christ today. Far too often we fault the devil for things we have permitted into our lives because of our own blindness. For example, we cannot fix blame on the enemy for the disintegration of our marriages if we have failed to fulfill our vows and live up to our marital contracts. We cannot blame the devil when our children go astray if we have neglected to raise them up in the fear and the admonition of the Lord. Those who pastor must not blame Satan when they lose their flocks if they have been too busy to hear the cry of their lambs when they were sick or when they were threatened by a wolf prowling in the night.

Satan can be a convenient scapegoat for failures caused by our own blindness. Although God is quick to forgive and ready to restore, nothing can be done until we see our handicapped condition, repent, and desire to be healed.

One of our greatest needs in order to escape spiritual disaster is discernment. It is the ability to perceive and evaluate things accurately, especially things in the spiritual realm. It is possessing good judgment and using it to separate right from wrong and good from evil. It is available only to those who are seeking God—those who are hungry and thirsty for the truth.

We learn discernment through experience,

but we also receive it from God as a gift. Time can make us wise and perceptive to the ways of life. The Holy Spirit also can illuminate our spirits and give us a supernatural understanding of the truth about a given situation. God can cause us to perceive what lies secluded behind the obvious. This is a gift that he gives to members of the body of Christ to keep us from being deceived. It is also a normal element of our spiritual growth. Whenever discernment is missing from Christ's people as a whole or from our individual lives, Satan and his forces take full advantage of our weaknesses by cunningly trying to weave a web of lies and counterfeit truths around us.

All believers need to have a certain measure of discernment, both to protect their own lives and to function effectively in the body of Christ. God never gives absolute discernment to any one person; doing so would set that person apart and would encourage independence rather than interdependence. Those who feel they have all the answers or that they have an ability to perceive things better than other believers are in grave danger of living as Pharisees. God has never entrusted total responsibility for the lives of others to any one human being alone. The Holy Spirit has reserved that right for himself.

Most of the good things that come from God can be counterfeited by the devil. We must pray regularly for discernment so that we can determine what is counterfeit and what is real. If we do not know how to recognize the voice of God, we are in danger of being deceived, because the leading of the Lord can be counterfeited by the enemy of our souls. This angel of light often produces such a close imitation of the real thing that even the most dedicated and devoted saints find it difficult at times to detect the difference between the voice of God and the voice of Satan. Jesus warned that "false christs and false prophets will rise and show signs and wonders to deceive, if possible, even the elect. But take heed" (Mark 13:22–23). Most of the time, we can detect the counterfeit and resist it. But to do this, we need to walk very closely with God and ask him to teach us by his Spirit what is real and what is false and deceptive.

As our discernment grows, we must not be surprised that things that seem sound and favorable on the surface do not always bring peace to our spirits. We must be sensitive to this feeling of uneasiness as a potential warning sign, and if a question still remains, we need to find safety in the additional discernment of other believers.

We must especially not allow the godly gift of discernment to become a stumbling block of suspicion. The devil delights in distracting God's people by causing them to feel a need to evaluate every person and situation that comes along. Fear and suspicion are not from the Lord and do not accompany a true spirit of discernment.

If we call upon the Lord and ask him for discernment, God says he will show us great and mighty things. When God shows us these things, we are guaranteed not to be deceived.

Dear Lord,
I know that my human mind is so limited. I can see and understand life based only on my own experiences, and I'm bound by a physical body in this life. Please lift me up higher to see and perceive correctly so that I might live a godly life in the Spirit. Help me to see things as you see them.

$\mathcal{K}$EEP ME

FROM ENVY

AND JEALOUSY

Plead my cause, O LORD, with those who strive with me; / Fight against those who fight against me.

(Ps. 35:1)

Do not fret because of evildoers, / Nor be envious of the workers of iniquity. / For they shall soon be cut down like the grass, / And wither as the green herb.

(Ps. 37:1–2)

*G*od has placed in each of us a motivation to achieve. We hunger for knowledge and understanding in order to build and create. Something inside our frame fires us to move the whole human race forward.

If we think about it for a moment, we can perceive this inner inspiration in many of the things we sense and feel. It's the drive that won't let us stop, because there is so much to be done. It's the feeling that we've got to get going in life because we have not yet arrived at our destination. It's an urge to go somewhere unique, to be somebody important, and to do something notable. It's a wonderful, compelling force, except that it has been damaged and perverted by Adam's sin. To strive for excellence is noble; to do so at the expense of another is sin.

Our basic problem is that we tend to use this propelling power in ways that injure other people. Individual excellence becomes a quest for superiority. Personal comparisons cause us to exalt ourselves while degrading others. In almost every situation in life we see ourselves in comparison to others. Every relational situation that we enter begins with an almost unconscious but real need to establish some kind of "pecking order." Our economic status, amount of education, and personal experiences all help us get established on a relational scale. And that is precisely where many of our problems begin.

Comparing ourselves with others is the root of envy and jealousy. This human tendency to look at other people with comparisons in mind is a voracious monster, a bottomless pit that is never satisfied. We indulge it by giving place to evil thoughts about others and by succumbing to gossip and slander. Envy and jealousy spring to life and stand ready to pounce on the person who is tempted to look at the wealth, fame, or position of another person with a lustful eye.

Asaph, King David's choir leader, fell prey to the evils of envy and jealousy. He began his story by saying, "Surely God is good to Israel, to those who are pure in heart. But as for me, my feet had almost slipped; I had nearly lost my foothold. For I envied the arrogant when I saw the prosperity of the wicked" (Ps. 73:1–3 NIV).

Asaph was an Old Testament Christian. He loved the Lord, but he had gotten tired and spiritually burned out. In his exhaustion he became confused and jealous when he noticed how materially prosperous unbelievers had become.

"They have no struggles," he continued, "Their bodies are healthy and strong. They are free from the burdens common to man; they are not plagued by human ills" (vv. 4–5). The carefree and reckless attitude of the world deceived him into evaluating incorrectly. As he gazed upon the wicked, he began to believe that they had some special blessing upon their lives.

Soon Asaph's self-deception led him to believe that his relationship with God had gotten him nowhere. "This is what the wicked are like—always carefree, they increase in wealth. Surely in vain have I kept my heart pure; in vain have I washed my hands in innocence" (vv. 12–13). All the energy he had poured into his faith appeared to be without profit.

"All day long I have been plagued; I have been punished every morning" (v. 14). At this point, self-pity had entered Asaph's heart. He felt he had been mistreated and that he deserved better than what he was getting; he deserved at least as much as those who make no effort to do right.

Further into the psalm, Asaph was still not sure how far to carry his feelings. "If I had said, 'I will speak thus,' I would have betrayed your children" (v. 15). Perhaps he was feeling a bit hypocritical because he was afraid that his true emotions would hurt other believers.

His confusion exhausted him until he couldn't bear to think about it any longer. His thoughts were making him depressed. Finally, he wandered into the house of the Lord and into his presence, where the truth suddenly became clear to him. "When I tried to understand all this, it was oppressive to me till I entered the sanctuary of God; then I understood their final destiny. Surely you place them on slippery ground; you cast them down to ruin. How suddenly are they destroyed, completely swept away by terrors!" (vv. 16–19).

Asaph finally was beginning to realize that he could not compare himself to others around him and that he needed to continue to trust God, who would make everything right in the end.

Envy and jealousy and the complaints that express these attitudes are always the result of comparisons. And when they are found in a Christian, they are an indictment against God. They accuse him of not being a good Father. They question his love for us and his concern for our personal needs and desires. We even begin to think that if

God really was good, he would treat us all fairly and equally.

Once the comparison game begins, complaints never cease. Murmuring soon develops into a negative spirit that persuades us that no one ever treats us right. Sadly, we never seem to be able to see the good things in life and rejoice in the blessings we do have. The joy of a thankful heart escapes us and we sink into the mire of self-pity.

God wants each of his children to stand alone before him. Because we all have distinct personalities and distinct functions in the body of Christ, he treats each of us uniquely. We wonder why he seems to bless one while withholding from another, but we must accept that reality if indeed we intend to obey him.

If we really believe that God does all things well, then we must believe that whatever he allows to happen in our lives will turn out all right in the end (Matt. 20:1–15). So we don't need to worry. Jesus said that if the Father cared for and fed the birds that fly through the air, he could easily care for and feed us, because we are more valuable than the birds. If God clothed the lilies of the field in such splendor, could he not just as easily clothe each of us (Matt. 6:25–34)? What do we have that

Keep Me from Envy and Jealousy

does not come from God? We need to recognize him as our source for everything in life.

If we are not careful, the problem continues when we drive into the church parking lot and most of the cars are better than the one we are driving. It's even worse when others are wearing nicer clothes than we are. No matter where we turn, someone else always has more material possessions than we have. That's all right; it's only temporary. The day is coming when God will make all things right.

We must be content to let others be ahead of us in everything in life except the graces of God. We need to work to be "first" in his kingdom with a heart of love, patience toward others, and hope in the midst of trouble.

Father God,
I thank you that I now understand that I stand alone before you in this world. I realize that it makes no difference what other people have or do in comparison to me. My personal obedience to you in the love relationship that you have established in Jesus is all that counts. Forgive me for looking so intently at the lives of others and for

harboring complaints in my heart as a result of feeling slighted by you and by others. Search my heart and show me any area of envy or jealousy that I may be cultivating against another person. Reveal any attitude of ungratefulness or lack of trust in you. Set me free from an unhealthy sense of self.

CHAPTER 11

GIVE ME

WISDOM AND

UNDERSTANDING

You have dealt well with Your servant, / O
LORD, according to Your word. / *Teach me
good judgment and knowledge, / For I believe
Your commandments.*

(Ps. 119:65–66)

*My son, if you receive my words, / And treasure
my commands within you, / So that you incline
your ear to wisdom, / And apply your heart to
understanding; ... If you seek her as silver, / And
search for her as for hidden treasures; / Then you
will understand the fear of the LORD, / And find*

the knowledge of God. / For the LORD gives
wisdom; / From His mouth come knowledge and
understanding.

(Prov. 2:1–6)

*M*ost of us want to be successful. We want to accomplish
something in life and enjoy the fulfillment that
comes from our achievement. And yet no matter
what heights we eventually attain, we never seem
to achieve enough. There always has to be more—
more fame, more power, more money, and more
of whatever it is that we think will make us happy.

For many of us, success and fulfillment are
somewhere up ahead. Real living is just around the
corner. The hope that someday things will be
better is what keeps many of us going.

When new ideas and inspirations come, we try
to believe that our great moment is about to happen. We dream that soon we will make it big in
life. Then there will be no more worries, no more
failures, and no more wishing things were better.
We reason that we can then rest a little at that
point because we will have finally "made it."

Made what? What is it that we are striving for?

Where is it that we want to go? And how will we know when we have arrived?

Whether or not we can nail down exactly what it is we are looking for in life, we do tend to believe one thing: that money will help us get what we want. The universal feeling is that money can solve most of our problems. And so our first priority is to get a lot of money.

Life then becomes a never-ending struggle to get ahead, to be successful, to attain power, and to get richer. Solomon, who in his day had every material thing imaginable, knew differently because he listened to wisdom.

"Receive my instruction," says wisdom, "and not silver, / And knowledge rather than choice gold; / For wisdom is better than rubies, / And all the things one may desire cannot be compared with her. / I, wisdom, dwell with prudence, / And find out knowledge and discretion" (Prov. 8:10–12). Solomon himself declared, "How much better to get wisdom than gold! / And to get understanding is to be chosen rather than silver!" (Prov. 16:16).

Could it really be that wisdom is more important than any other thing we could strive for in life other than God? Could wisdom be more important than making a living, or finding fulfillment in a relationship, or becoming a renowned and well-respected person? Is it possible that wisdom should be our first priority in life next to God himself? Solomon seemed to think so, according to this passage in Proverbs:

> *Get wisdom! Get understanding! / Do not forget, nor turn away from the words of my mouth. / Do not forsake her, and she will preserve you; / Love her, and she will keep you. / Wisdom is the principal thing; / Therefore get wisdom. / And in all your getting, get understanding. / Exalt her, and she will promote you; / She will bring you honor, when you embrace her. / She will place on your head an ornament of grace; / A crown of glory she will deliver to you* (Prov. 4:5–9).

Instead of seeking wisdom, however, we tend to pursue personal achievement in order to reach permanent heights of happiness and contentment. When we do this, we never come close to our true desires, for all that we find in this world is only a cheap imitation for what we really need. A prestigious job, intellectual pride in years of education, and the fame and fortune that come from such environments as the arts and entertainment industry provide only temporary fulfillment. These act as counterfeit answers and are similar to trying repeatedly to jam the wrong latchkeys into the locked-up areas of our lives. No matter how hard we try or how much energy and determination we exert, the door will not open.

Will more self-effort enable us to reach new heights of success or esteem? Will our appetites ever be satisfied, or are we waging a losing battle with insatiable human needs and desires that can never be filled by anyone but God alone?

Why do we continue to dip our cups into the cisterns of vain human thinking and reasoning, knowing that the contents are polluted and are not for our use or consumption? While searching for more depth of caring and concern from other human beings, are we not really searching for the depths and heights of God's love for us? While chasing after admiration and respect in the world's social system, are we not crying out for God's unconditional approval and acceptance of us?

This seemingly endless search for ultimate security and safety is found in God alone. How, then, do we find the answers, the wisdom and understanding, to quell our fears and bring clarity to our lives? James 1:5 says, "If any of you lacks wisdom, let him ask of God, who gives to all liberally and without reproach, and it will be given to him." Asking, then, is the first step.

Next, we must develop a deep respect for the Lord. "The fear of the LORD is the beginning of wisdom, / And the knowledge of the Holy One is understanding" (Prov. 9:10). "The fear of the LORD is the instruction of wisdom, / And before honor is humility" (Prov. 15:33).

The basis of this reverential fear of God is our adoration and worship of him—our deep and devoted affection for him. God does not want us to live in terror of him nor in dread of his presence. That's not what the fear of the Lord is all about. We are to delight ourselves in him, finding joy as we discover his attributes, while at the same time cultivating a reverent respect for him.

All of us want to be happy and blessed. Wisdom will see to it that we are. "Happy is the man who finds wisdom, / And the man who gains understanding" (Prov. 3:13). We begin to get wisdom, then, by reverencing and esteeming God. That means paying attention to him. By looking to him, we add wisdom to our lives. We do this mainly by honoring his Word, obeying his commandments, and respecting other people.

As God's people, then, we are to be "seekers." We are on a quest, traveling along hidden paths. We are given divine and sacred fruit to eat that changes our perspective and our very character.

When we meet those who have sought wisdom by seeking the Lord, we find very unusual individuals.

They are sensitive to the needs of others.

They choose their words carefully so that they communicate effectively, without causing confusion.

Their speech is clean and uplifting.

They share conversation rather than dominate it.

Their demeanor is characterized by a quiet and gentle spirit.

When offended they do not retaliate.

Their lives are marked by purity.

They are approachable.

Mercy and forgiveness are always near them.

They guard against hypocrisy.

They are peacemakers.

They distinguish between right and wrong without partiality.

They follow the soundest course of action.

Their meekness is never perceived as weakness.

Good humor and a gentle smile make them pleasant to be around.

The will of the Lord is always on their minds.

They recognize that the moment a word leaves their mouths, they are responsible for it.

When bad things happen, they are not quick to find blame.

They add to the lives of others.

And the good that comes from them is motivated by love, not by compulsion.

All of these things come from being in God's presence, which is the same as being in the presence of all wisdom, for God is wisdom personified.

God, our Father, is extending an open-ended invitation to all of us to seek him out and to ask him for wisdom and understanding. We do not need to waste precious time and energy by striving to find the answers in our own fleshly knowledge and experiences. The answers are found in God. He alone is the master locksmith. He will provide each of us with the correct key to fit into the troublesome locks of our lives. His perfectly designed key will be the solution and the appropriate answer for all of our problems and questions.

> *Dearest Lord,*
> *All too often I find myself at some crossroad, unable to determine any real direction in life. I cry out to you to let me see clearly which road to travel. I desire to know your ways and to honor you with my life. Without your wisdom and direction I cannot do what my heart longs to do. I worship you and wait for the answers that will quench the deep thirsting of my soul. I know you will not ignore my cry or forsake my need for help. I reach out to you as a child reaches out to a parent. I wait patiently for your answers.*

CHAPTER 12

EACH ME

TO PRAY

Give ear to my words, O LORD, / Consider my meditation. / Give heed to the voice of my cry, / My King and my God, / For to You I will pray.

(Ps. 5:1–2)

"Offer to God thanksgiving, / And pay your vows to the Most High. / Call upon Me in the day of trouble; / I will deliver you, and you shall glorify Me."

(Ps. 50:14–15)

Sermons on prayer are helpful and encouraging. Books on prayer are inspiring. But the only way we will ever learn to pray is by actually praying.

Do we desire a better and more fulfilling prayer life? Then we must enroll in the school of prayer. There the Holy Spirit will teach us to pray. Under his instruction and guidance we will find that practice and persistence unite to produce a loving and intimate relationship with the Father. In his presence, prayer becomes more than a brief few moments of reciting "grace" at the dinner table or a thought or two quickly turned heavenward in those short moments before bedtime.

Most Christians do believe in prayer, and most of us pray. But we don't pray very much, and we don't pray very effectively. That is evident by our own confession. Busyness, preoccupation with the cares of life, a wandering mind, and numerous other demands and hindrances rob us from the most valuable part of our day—time spent alone with Father God.

Whatever our need may be for an improved time in prayer, we will find a struggle with both quality and quantity. But neither quality nor quantity is very significant if we don't understand that prayer is much more than presenting a list of requests to God. Many Christians mistakenly believe prayer to be a way to manipulate God, reducing him to a cosmic vending machine. We put a quarter's worth of prayer in, and out comes what we requested. To others, prayer is a "superstitious" act to stave off bad luck or to promote blessings like those that are supposed to come by stroking a rabbit's foot. Some people perceive God as a principle and never really get to know him as a person. Some people serve religious ethics and morality, thinking that they are serving God. And while wholesome living is important, it was never meant to be a substitute for a personal, intimate relationship with God through prayer.

These incorrect concepts of prayer distract us from the target—God's deep desire for communion with his people. Prayer is part of our relationship with God; it is a communication system with the Father, who is our Friend and Counselor. Simply put, prayer is talking with God. Through this system flow praise, worship, thanksgiving, confession, meditation, listening, and eventually intercession, which is the kind of power-filled prayer that shakes the enemy's kingdom. Power, authority, comfort, assurance, and guidance flow back to the believer through this system, and especially through the Word of God. These benefits of prayer affect our own lives and the lives of others as well.

The full expression and potential of prayer

becomes evident when we pray because of a developing passion for God. Our perspective, and especially the amount of time we spend in prayer, gain new meaning when our primary quest is to truly know God and not to merely obtain something from him. As we reach the destination of our quest, we realize the ultimate design of prayer—to know God. It was not ordained as a means to earn or gain favor or special privileges from God. It is a means of producing a relationship that thrives on time spent together. And spending time with someone is the only way to really get to know that person.

In spending time alone with God in prayer, we discover the secret to answered prayer. Contrary to some thinking, the secret to answered prayer does not begin with great faith. It begins with our love for God, a love that develops as we truly get to know him. *"Because he has set his love upon me,"* says the Lord, "therefore I will deliver him; / I will set him on high, because he has known My name. / He shall call upon Me, and I will answer him; / I will be with him in trouble; / I will deliver him and honor him" (Ps. 91:14–15). In this case, why does God say he will answer prayer? Because of love for him!

If prayer were not so important to our loving

and abiding relationship with God—as well as destructive to the influences of the enemy in our lives—we would not experience so many obstacles diverting us from it. When we make a daily commitment to prayer, we quickly note the hindrances. Doubt, weariness, distractions, and a host of other interferences come running like a pack of little foxes when we decide to give ourselves to prayer.

And far too many of us give up on prayer, not because we are not sincerely interested, but because of these distractions and personal attacks from the enemy. The devil will do everything possible to destroy this most valuable part of our day and our lives, while suggesting to us that God is responsible for not protecting us in the midst of our new dedication to prayer.

Prayer is also hindered by disobedience. Sometimes people who are hurt and are angry with God refuse to serve him because a particular prayer was not answered.

God yearns for us to cooperate in developing a close and abiding relationship with him. Especially when we are hurt and disappointed, we must turn to God to maintain a flow of communication. In those times of prayer, burdens are lifted, hopes and desires are encouraged, broken hearts are mended, wisdom and knowledge are imparted—but most important, our friendship with God is deepened and becomes anchored in love. Such a life of prayer takes time, and suffers momentarily at the hands of discouragement. But we must never give up.

A note of caution: We must be careful about what we hear in a moment of prayer. God will never speak anything to us that does not agree with his Word. And he seldom speaks a truth, a direction, or even a rebuke in a sudden flash to our minds. He usually plants a seed deep within us, where it slowly moves into our thoughts and then grows into understanding. The enemy of our souls speaks to our minds, hoping to get his own thoughts deeply imbedded in our spirits.

If we want to know God and hear him accurately, we must spend time with him. Running in and out of his presence hurriedly is of little worth to a deep and abiding relationship. The knowledge we get from him comes in small bits and pieces over extended periods of time. We must take courage even if the process seems slow. A child cannot be taught many great things in a single session. Likewise, it takes time for us to get to know God.

Dear Lord,
Like the disciples who asked you to teach them to
pray, I also ask for your help in learning to pray.
I want to pray, but so often I am distracted by
other things. Sometimes the problem is that you
seem distant, and it's hard to feel that you really
care about me. I want to know you. Please help
me.

CHAPTER 13

ℋELP ME TO LOVE

THE THINGS YOU LOVE

AND HATE THE

THINGS YOU HATE

I love Your commandments / More than gold, yes, than fine gold! / Therefore all Your precepts concerning all things / I consider to be right; / I hate every false way.

(Ps. 119:127–128)

"For I, the LORD, love justice; / I hate robbery. . . ."

(Isa. 61:8)

To really understand what God loves, we need to know also what he hates. He loves truth and hates lying. He loves life and hates death. He loves light and hates darkness. In reality, he loves love and hates hate.

Sadly, the things that God loves are not always the things that we love. Likewise, the things that God hates are not always the things that we hate.

We despise the things that cause us unhappiness and the things and situations that frighten us. But God, the Father, is not moved by fear or apprehension, nor is he manipulated or swayed by circumstances. Nothing can make him become inconsistent or unstable. All the earth and its inhabitants were made for his pleasure, and he isn't frightened by any of the things he has created. He is not fearful of darkness, and he has no sin or shame to cause him to feel uncomfortable in the light. And so the things we hate are often different from the things God hates.

What is it, then, that God hates? Proverbs 6:16–19 lists seven things:

- God hates haughty eyes. He finds no pleasure in the proud look of a person who wants to be exalted above others.

- God hates a lying tongue. Lies damage relationships and destroy happiness, peace, and joy.

- God hates hands that shed innocent blood. He created us to be at peace with one another, not to destroy each other.

- God hates a heart that devises wicked plans. The root of wickedness is the desire to promote and exalt oneself at the expense or even destruction of another person.

- God hates feet that are swift in running to evil. Some people have consciences that are seared and indifferent toward what is good and right. These people run quickly, whenever possible, to satisfy their own insatiable lusts and desires, and have little or no regard for others.

- God hates a false witness who speaks lies. The person who loses moral and ethical character cannot be trusted with the truth, and nothing that comes out of that person's mouth can be relied upon as true.

- God hates those who stir up dissension among their brothers and sisters.

It is important to understand that God hates the evil that such people commit, and not the people themselves. That is evident in his desire to forgive us when we are willing to confess and forsake our sin. At the same time, we must recognize that God's anger is kindled and directed against those who revel in quarreling and finding fault with the body of Christ. They criticize and judge so sanctimoniously that any Pharisee would be proud to call them his brothers and sisters. God's heart is deeply grieved by such behavior, especially with those believers who have no apparent desire to see things made right and to see Christ's body edified and strengthened.

All seven of these issues that point to God's displeasure are associated with relationships. Anything that destroys a right relationship with God or with other people is something that he abhors. Always keep in mind that the foundation of all of

God's commandments pertains to relationships and God's desire for his people to be wholesome and healthy together. Remember, everything in the Law and all that the prophets spoke can be summed up in two such commandments: You shall love the Lord, and you shall love others.

Sin, quite simply, is anything that either offends God or hurts others. To share in God's hatred of those sins, we must first have a heart like God's and a perspective that is able to rise above earthly circumstances so that we see things as God sees them. We attain these when we establish a close relationship with God in prayer and daily living.

What does God love? We can sum it up in one word: *people*. We can use the word *world* in place of *people* as long as we understand that the word includes you and me as individuals in a very personal sense.

But God's love doesn't appear evident when we look at the sad, degenerative condition of our world. It's easy to assume that if he really loved us he wouldn't allow such suffering and sorrow among us. Where, then, is the proof of God's love in today's world? It is in the cross!

Indeed, God loved us so much that he put heaven at risk in order to save us. God, in Jesus, literally became flesh himself. He put himself in a position in which he would suffer, experience temptation, and face all of the perplexing problems common to every one of us. Perhaps there was no other way that we would believe that God really cared for us than for him to prove it by suffering the same things that we suffer and by sacrificing his own life for ours.

But why did God bother to prove his love? Could he not have arbitrarily demanded that we be obedient and good? Why didn't he just put down all sin with an absolute forceful command?

If he had done so, he would have violated our free will. In the process, all of the uniqueness and precious individuality that he had so carefully placed within each of us would have been destroyed. So his solution to destroying evil and its ability to produce suffering and sorrow had to begin by winning us back to himself. And he could do that only by convincing us of his deep, gracious love and his pure motives. We see God's love, then, in his willingness to give as much as he did in the redemption process.

Just how much did he give? That is a theological question worthy of much debate. Is it possible that God gave so much that, at the time, he placed

Help Me to Love the Things You Love . . .

heaven at risk? In other words, could God have failed in his mission? If, in fact, failure was possible, we are looking at unimaginable love. If he couldn't have failed, it is questionable that there was any substance to what he suffered. His temptations, then, could not be called temptations—for to be tempted implies the ability to fail. If, indeed, God went so far in his effort to rescue us and to prove his love for us that he could have failed, then he is far more worthy of our praise and adoration than most of us can imagine.

Regardless of the theology of the risk in rescuing lost humanity, God still has good reason in calling his children to love others. It is because he gave so liberally of his love. But we cannot love like that until we have experienced his love. Tasting God's love has the power to change our views, heal our emotional wounds, and eradicate deep feelings of shame and failure that result from past sins committed by us or against us. God's love mends broken hearts, removes scar tissue from within the soul, and turns hearts of stone into warm, pulsating, vitally alive, loving hearts like that of Father God. That kind of God-inspired love makes us willing to sacrifice our lives for others. "Greater love has no one than this, than to lay down one's life for his friends" (John 15:13).

This human display of sacrificial love is impossible until we've seen and experienced the love of God in our own lives. That is why the cross is so important. Nothing in human history illustrates so radiantly the depth, width, and length of God's love than the cross. Not only is it the place God has chosen to destroy the sin that he hates, but it is also the starting point for love. Until we are able to behold and embrace the cross, we are capable only of limited conditional love.

Father God,
Help me to see things as you see them, to hear as
you hear, to love as you love, and to hate as you
hate. Help me to progressively understand the
true meaning of the cross. May it always remind
me of your love.

$\mathcal{H}$ELP ME TO

DWELL PEACEFULLY

WITH YOUR PEOPLE

Behold, how good and how pleasant it is / For brethren to dwell together in unity!

(Ps. 133:1)

If it is possible, as much as depends on you, live peaceably with all men. Beloved, do not avenge yourselves, but rather give place to wrath; for it is written, "Vengeance is Mine, I will repay," says the Lord. Therefore / "If your enemy is hungry, feed him; / If he is thirsty, give him a drink; / For in so doing you will heap coals of fire on his head." / Do not be

overcome by evil, but overcome evil with
good.

(Rom. 12:18–21)

*D*id God create human beings
to be self-contained and self-
sufficient? Or did he desire for his creation to relate
to him and to other human beings in deep and
meaningful ways?

One of God's primary messages to us is that
believers need each other. "For in fact the body is
not one member but many. If the foot should say,
'Because I am not a hand, I am not of the body,' is
it therefore not of the body? . . . If one member
suffers, all the members suffer with it; or if one
member is honored, all the members rejoice with
it" (1 Cor. 12:14–15, 26).

We must never forget that "no man is an island," that we were not meant to be alone, and that
we need each other. God's desire is to provide
safety, protection, and blessing in a *company* of
believers. Satan's demons work overtime to pro-
voke sins of slander, backbiting, gossip, hatred, and
a host of other destructive attitudes and actions
designed to destroy the body of Christ. As a result,

God's people are isolated from each other and are left vulnerable to more insidious attacks by the enemy. And the enemy takes full advantage of these moments of discord in our relationships to generate resentments and bitternesses that separate and destroy. We don't have to be at sword points with each other too often before we simply want to be left alone. Before long, we are vulnerable to loneliness and rejection, which in turn give place to worry, anxiety, fear, discouragement, and depression. Soon we find our own mental, emotional, and spiritual health in jeopardy.

If we check our prayer lives to see how many of our prayers are being answered, we may find that more answers are coming as others are praying for us than when we pray alone. We may also find that as we pray for others, their prayers are answered much more readily as well. Why is this so? Does God need large numbers of prayers directed toward heaven before he acts? Or is there another reason? Is it possible that God wants us to pray for each other so that we are not tempted to try to make it through life on our own? Sharing our troubles and concerns with one another provides part of the fellowship needed to maintain a healthy existence. It keeps us from becoming separated from others, so that evils such as loneliness and rejection do not find fertile ground in which to grow.

If God answered all of our personal prayers without the assistance of brothers and sisters in Christ, we wouldn't need our brothers and sisters. The potential for pride at that point would give Satan an added advantage in his attempts to destroy us.

The enemy finds it more difficult to overwhelm and subdue us with attacks upon our minds when we continually allow God's Spirit to edify us and strengthen us through the many members in Christ's body. This is a powerful reason why praying for and encouraging one another is so vitally important.

As most seasoned believers can attest, we don't have to encounter very many Christian relationships to experience hurt and disappointment. Human frailties abound, and our inhumanity toward each other happens all too often. But determined "seekers of peace," although troubled and often hurt by these regretful and disheartening trials, are not defeated.

Paul spoke a great deal of the need for building up one another. Unlike Jonah, Paul did not excuse himself from this task, believing that people were unworthy of being built up. Paul could look tolerantly and with mercy past the faults of many, knowing that he was, as he put it, the "chief of sinners." He never justified sin, but he was very aware that all humankind is justified when we present our sins to Christ and repent.

While in this body of clay, we will always be plagued by our inclination to sin. For us to acknowledge this problem is not a resignation to hopelessness and condemnation but an honest evaluation of our condition. As believers we are to be mindful of our fragile frame and its inherent weaknesses.

Paul possessed the kind of heart that hates sin while still loving the sinner. Most of us have trouble making the distinction. If we remain unenlightened and ignorant of God's great grace, we become shallow critics, and we will constantly be disappointed with other Christians. No one will ever live as uprightly as we arbitrarily judge they should.

The greatest message from God to the body of Christ is that we should love one another. And yet we often find ourselves terribly fragmented and divided—lacking the unity and harmony that the Bible speaks of. There is only one reason why we find it so difficult to get along with our brothers and sisters: we have yet to know God as a close Friend. We may be saved, but our salvation has not yet been consummated to produce an intimacy with God that makes us faithful, loyal, obedient, and loving children of the Father.

God's concern about the way we treat one another is clear. "Bear one another's burdens, and so fulfill the law of Christ" (Gal. 6:2). "Let no corrupt word proceed out of your mouth, but what is good for necessary edification, that it may impart grace to the hearers" (Eph. 4:29). "Submit to one another out of reverence for Christ" (Eph. 5:21 NIV). "Let nothing be done through selfish ambition or conceit, but in lowliness of mind let each esteem others better than himself. Let each of you look out not only for his own interests, but also for the interests of others" (Phil. 2:3–4). "Therefore, as the elect of God, holy and beloved, put on tender mercies, kindness, humility, meekness, longsuffering; bearing with one another, and forgiving one another, if anyone has a complaint against another; even as Christ forgave you, so you also must do. But above all these things, put on love, which is the bond of perfection" (Col. 3:12–14).

Jesus has called us to unpretentious service and

genuine humility. It's true that we are to be obedient to the commands of God, but laws and precepts alone can be heartless unless they contain the warmth of genuine love. We need to remember again that all of the Law and the Prophets can be summed up in two commandments—to love God and to love others.

As disciples of Jesus, we must be careful to guard our own hearts. The subtle unloving attitudes of the legalists of Jesus' day can creep into our own souls just as a thief sneaks into a house to steal.

We must know the Word of God concerning our relationships with others, but that knowledge alone does not fully equip us to love. To love as God loves requires an encounter with God himself. We must personally and privately experience Father God's love for ourselves. We need to perceive with our minds the beauty of his limitless grace, mercy, and love, but we must allow those things to also seep into all the deep crevices of our hearts and souls.

Intimate encounters with God produce divine attributes in his children. Through these encounters we become gracious, loving, and forgiving people who desire wholesome relationships—people who work hard for reconciliation and restoration when things have deteriorated. After spending time with God, we cannot help becoming lovers of God and lovers of humankind.

Father God,
Help me always to remember that pure and undefiled religion is expressed in helping others. As you meet my needs, may I ever be conscious to reach out and meet the needs of others.

CHAPTER 15

*R*EMIND

ME TO BE

THANKFUL

Bless the LORD, O my soul, / *And forget not all His benefits.*

(Ps. 103:2)

Be anxious for nothing, but in everything by prayer and supplication, with thanksgiving, let your requests be made known to God.

(Phil. 4:6)

*O*ne of the most challenging lessons in life is to develop an attitude of thankfulness. The posture of our hearts toward God and toward our fellow human beings is of great importance if we are to truly appreciate all the blessings bestowed upon us. Thanksgiving is a necessary material for building strong ties with both God and other people. Words of appreciation are as important to a relationship as fine furnishings are to an elegant room.

True thankfulness bows the heart before another person with a sentiment of loving respect. It says, "I appreciate what you have done for me." Having a grateful heart means acknowledging and honoring those who give to us. And yet we occasionally find it a very difficult task to practice.

At times it is difficult to be grateful and to focus on our blessings, especially when they are obscured by the debris of life. We can become so self-absorbed and preoccupied that we fail to notice and give proper appreciation to God, our caring Father, and to the people around us who love us.

Often it is only by losing something or someone we truly cherish that we begin to appreciate the things formerly taken for granted. We usually appreciate the beauty of a friendship only after the friend is gone. Appreciation finds new meaning when the blessings of yesterday are only a mem-

Remind Me to Be Thankful   *115*

ory. Those who have suffered loss the most may be those who more often tend to develop a profound gratitude for all that they do have. They are able to sift quickly through life's rubble and find their treasures.

If we have food on our tables, clothes on our backs, shelter over our heads, and good health, we can be very thankful. But we are apt to lose our sense of appreciation when we compare our condition with that of others. Once our attention is diverted from our own blessings and onto the blessings of others, we are in danger of becoming resentful and eventually bitter. No matter how much we have, we may have trouble with thankfulness if we focus on the blessings of others.

Many of us tend to take the good things in life for granted, and instead of being thankful for what we have, we become dissatisfied. We are like the fire that consumes with ravenous hunger but is never satisfied, or the ocean that drinks up the rivers but is always thirsty. Once our minds are flooded with reasons to be ungrateful, we become blinded to the provisions and blessings that God supplies to us.

The problem is not that we *need* so much in life, it is that we *want* so much. Yet in getting things, we never seem to get enough. And so we never stop to count our blessings and be thankful.

Why do we toil so hard to get things when there is nothing we can take with us when we die? "As he came from his mother's womb, naked shall he return, / To go as he came; / And he shall take nothing from his labor / Which he may carry away in his hand" (Eccl. 5:15). Solomon concluded that "there is a man whose labor is with wisdom, knowledge, and skill; yet he must leave his heritage to a man who has not labored for it" (Eccl. 2:21). "And who knows whether he will be wise or a fool? Yet he will rule over all my labor in which I toiled and in which I have shown myself wise under the sun" (Eccl. 2:19).

This world constantly emphasizes the need for fulfillment. It offers false and unsatisfying delicacies that soon lose their flavor. What remains is an undefinable gnawing in the soul. Nothing ever seems to gratify or bring contentment. It is at this juncture that we must be a people who seek the kingdom of God and not the prized treasures of the world.

We begin to be thankful when we recognize and acknowledge the things we already possess, regardless of whether someone else has more. A grateful heart grows well when it is watered with contentment. The apostle Paul wrote to Timothy that "godliness with contentment is great gain. For we brought nothing into this world, and it is certain we can carry nothing out. And having food and clothing, with these we shall be content. But those who desire to be rich fall into temptation and a snare, and into many foolish and harmful lusts which drown men in destruction and perdition" (1 Tim. 6:6–9).

A thankful attitude deepens our satisfaction. This truth is emphasized in Ecclesiastes 2:24–26:

Nothing is better for a man than that he should eat and drink, and that his soul should enjoy good in his labor. This also, I saw, was from the hand of God. For who can eat, or who can have enjoyment, more than I? For God gives wisdom and knowledge and joy to a man who is good in His sight, but to the sinner He gives the work of gathering and collecting, that he may give to him who is good before God.

Taking things for granted helps to develop the sin of unthankfulness. There may be times when what we do for others goes unnoticed. At that point it's hard to continue giving of our time, energy, or material goods when we are not recognized or appreciated. In the same manner we must not lose sight of what God and others are doing to bless our lives and honor them with our thankfulness.

Relationships need to be cultivated and nurtured with gracious attitudes and thoughtful deeds. Just as a delicate flower needs to be watered and handled with gentleness and care, so also those in our lives who have given to us need to be nurtured.

A grateful heart is a sign of maturity. It is a characteristic that Father God longs to see manifested in us. Kindness, consideration, and compassion grow well in gardens watered often with thankfulness. These traits not only glorify God but tenderly invite others to meet and experience him also.

Throughout God's Word is a strong thread of grace and love. If we ask the Lord to open our eyes to behold all that he has done in us and for us, that thread will redefine the meaning and purpose of our lives and create in us greater thanksgiving. Rather than questioning why so many things are wrong

Remind Me to Be Thankful   *119*

and even our reason for living, we will find ourselves enjoying an intimate relationship with him.

The apostle Paul eloquently exhorts the Philippians by saying, "Do all things without complaining and disputing, that you may become blameless and harmless, children of God without fault in the midst of a crooked and perverse generation, among whom you shine as lights in the world" (Phil. 2:14–15).

Father God,
May my eyes ever be opened to see the blessings that surround me daily. Even in the midst of severe trials may I always be mindful that there are things to be grateful for.

CHAPTER 16

*L*ET ME

DWELL DAILY

IN YOUR PRESENCE

One thing I have desired of the LORD, / That will I seek: / *That I may dwell in the house of the LORD / All the days of my life, / To behold the beauty of the LORD,* / And to inquire in His temple.

(Ps. 27:4)

For I know the thoughts that I think toward you, says the LORD, thoughts of peace and not of evil, to give you a future and a hope. Then you will call upon Me and go and pray to Me, and I will listen to you. *And you will*

seek Me and find Me, when you search for Me
with all your heart.

(Jer. 29:11–13)

*I*f the Scriptures truly teach that humankind was created for fellowship with God, then the human heart can be satisfied with nothing less than union with God himself. If our Creator desired and intended to have a closeness with his creation as in the marriage relationship described in the book of Revelation, then we must prepare ourselves and be properly adorned as a bride readies herself to meet her bridegroom.

Of all the things that may hinder this relationship, nothing is so destructive as our own determination to find happiness and fulfillment outside God himself. The fallen sin nature of all humankind produces an antagonism toward God and believes the worst about him before it believes the best. Because we cannot answer the question 'How can a good God allow such suffering and sorrow in our world?' we fall prey to the misconception that he is not a good and loving God. Because we often do not hear from him in the way we expect or with the frequency we desire, we think that he does not care about us or regard our needs and concerns as important.

God's love couldn't penetrate the hardness of the human soul until he personally stepped onto the stage of human drama to sacrificially suffer and die. From his birth to his death on the cross there is one single, unmistakable message, "For God so loved the world."

Many of life's plaguing questions will not be answered this side of heaven. That, however, must not keep us from seeking after and finding the love of God. Sadly, it is at this juncture that many disappointed and disheartened people cease their journey to search out God's dwelling place. They distance themselves from the Giver of Life. Most of us want God on our own terms, which is a stumbling block to salvation and intimacy with him. God declares that Jesus is the only doorway into his presence, and yet we attempt thousands of other ways to enter in.

Fortunately for us, God's love continues to be directed toward us even though we refuse it. This is the wondrous nature of God himself: he loves us in our fragile human condition. Father God waits patiently for us to exhaust all mortal resources so that we might finally realize that real living is found only in a love relationship with him. Only when the walls between ourselves and God are broken down and we begin to know him, only when we have tasted of his love, do we find that this earthly, temporal life cannot substitute or satisfy the cry in our souls for God. The things of life grow uniquely dim in his radiant presence. When people truly find God, they realize that he is what they have been searching for all of their lives.

Many people will insist that the God of the universe cannot be apprehended and that we certainly cannot know him personally. They do not believe that intimacy with him is possible this side of the grave. But millions of people will testify differently. They have diligently and persistently sought him in prayer and through his Word, and as a result have begun to really know him. They have not been disappointed or disillusioned and can attest that Father God truly is merciful, kind, and full of grace, and that his love endures forever.

Much of the joy derived from dwelling in God's presence comes from discovering his marvelous attributes. To feel and experience his gentleness and patience is an awesome revelation, especially to those of us who previously believed that God possessed an explosive temper and a heavy hand of disapproval and condemnation. An outgrowth of this revelation is finding that Father God cares about all our needs, our feelings, and our hopes and dreams. We can find comfort in his presence and receive counsel and direction for our most confusing dilemmas and predicaments. His desire as our Father is for his children to feel safe enough to crawl up into his lap and into his arms with our fears, our needs, our requests, and our hearts. There he becomes our Abba Father, our "Daddy God."

Some people may feel it is childish to approach God as anything but sophisticated adults in full control of their own lives. That is where many lose their way. Father God invites us to be child*like*—to be real, without guile or deceit. When we are in his presence he will heal our childish ways, our immaturity, our foolishness, and even our lack of faith in him. It is there, in those quiet and tender moments of intimacy, that we find the deep, enduring love that no human being can supply. Just as a child cries out to its earthly father and is loved and cared for, so also our heavenly Father will not abandon us or disregard our childlike cries for help. Our God desires that kind of close, consummate, open, and communicative relationship with us. He is waiting. He is ready and available when we are.

In speaking to the Lord, the psalmist affirmed, "A day in your courts is better than a thousand. / I would rather be a doorkeeper in the house of my God / Than dwell in the tents of wickedness. / For the LORD God is a sun and shield; / The LORD will give grace and glory; / No good thing will He withhold / From those who walk uprightly" (Ps. 84:10–11).

Dear God,
I desire a close, special relationship with you. For-
give me for my pride, my stubborn ways, and the
busyness that keeps me from seeking you. Change
me so that you become the most important person
in my life. As I abide in your presence, heal me of
my childish ways and help me to become childlike
before you. May I never stop seeking you all the
days of my life.

CHAPTER 17

*K*EEP

MY TONGUE

FROM EVIL

Set a guard, O LORD, over my mouth; / Keep watch over the door of my lips.

(Ps. 141:3)

If anyone does not stumble in word, he is a perfect man, able also to bridle the whole body.

(James 3:2)

*W*e are wise to assess how our words touch others. The words that proceed from our lips can defile and bring death or else they can bless, heal, and create abundant life. Our tongues can be used as sharply edged weapons that drive people away, often leaving behind broken hearts and ravaged emotions, or they can uplift and strengthen the lives of those who hear them.

Words have the power to erect walls to shut others out or to lovingly invite others into our lives. Gentle words embrace another soul with love. Compassionate words are like a soothing balm to an aching heart. Without these kind and tender words, hearts are crushed and relationships are shattered.

Many of our troubles in life come from the misuse of the tongue. James, in writing to the Church, describes the tongue as "a fire, a world of iniquity. The tongue is so set among our members that it defiles the whole body, and sets on fire the course of nature; and it is set on fire by hell" (James 3:6).

If we are to guard our hearts and our tongues, we need to beware of the following dangers:

A lying tongue. Some people seem to have no conscience when it comes to telling the truth.

They seem compelled to fulfill their own needs and desires, even to the detriment and expense of others. Their own personal gain is their first priority. How different it becomes when Jesus enters someone's life and that person begins to tell the truth.

A spurious tongue. From the spurious tongue come forth eloquent lies, carefully designed and constructed fallacies, and counterfeit truths. The hearts of such people are deceitful and evasive, and their words are empty—void of any real love or compassion.

A foolish, jesting tongue. This tongue uses insensitive jesting, sarcasm, and mockery to belittle others. The result is damaged emotions and ruined relationships. "I was only joking" is a cheap excuse aimed at glossing over words that cut deeply into the life of another person. Once they are spoken, hurtful words cannot be taken back. They cause injury to the character and feelings of others, and they show disrespect and unkindness.

A self-centered tongue. Those who have this kind of tongue are chronically preoccupied with self. Their conversations are limited to their own concerns, and they show little interest in others.

A fearful tongue. Some people are waging daily

warfare against fear. That struggle permeates all they say and do.

An evil tongue. Profanity is common almost anywhere we turn in our world. God's name and character are often casually blasphemed, and those who participate in this activity are frequently unaware of it until it is mentioned.

An angry tongue. Rage and fury empower the tongue and make it an instrument of abuse that cuts deep into the souls of others. Often unforgiveness and unresolved hurts cause anger to manifest in our communication and in our treatment of others.

A deceitful tongue. The tongue of a deceptive person drips with intentional lies and misrepresentations. This deception evolves from a heart that is filled with guile and treachery. As a result, this person betrays almost all of his or her relationships.

A divisive tongue. We must be careful to avoid making slanderous and accusatory statements about others. A divisive tongue can cast doubt upon the character of another person. Offhanded slanderous remarks, innuendos that put other people and institutions in a bad light, and negative comments that are meant to ruin other people are all marks of a person who is being used by Satan to destroy others.

A proud tongue. Pride has at its core the desire not only to exalt the proud person in indulgent egotism but also to debase another person in order to appear superior. Satan's bid to be like God was motivated by his pride and his desire to dominate all that God had created. That same perverted aspiration still drives people today. Our preoccupation with success and our frenzied attempts to acquire more money and possessions are the product of pride and its subsequent need for control.

Most of the problems of life begin with our tongues. Our only hope to avoid such problems is to ask God to cleanse our hearts so that our tongues bring forth wholeness and rightness.

Father God,
As I think about these sins of the tongue, I can see
places where I have failed. My tongue has not al-
ways spoken words that glorify you and express
care and concern for others. Forgive me, and help
me to listen carefully to what I say so that my
words become sweet and wholesome.

$\mathscr{T}$EACH ME

TO BE

GENEROUS

The wicked borrows and does not repay, /
But *the righteous shows mercy and gives.*

(Ps. 37:21)

"Give, and it will be given to you: good measure,
pressed down, shaken together, and running
over will be put into your bosom. For with
the same measure that you use, it will be
measured back to you."

(Luke 6:38)

*T*he act of giving is foundational to all relationships. We all have a need to give of our lives and to receive from the lives of others. As necessary as good, nourishing food and clean, unpolluted air are to the human body, so are close, wholesome relationships to the soul. God did not create us to dwell alone; we need one another. Therefore, it is important that we invest ourselves in the lives of others.

Beneficial relationships require that we liberally give of our time, of our energy, of our financial resources, and most importantly of our hearts. Father God created us to be relational beings; we are dependent on both God and other people. When friendship and camaraderie are lacking, we find that life is lonely, melancholy, and unfulfilling.

Relationships thrive and grow as a result of our personal, heartfelt involvement in the lives of others. The strength of any good friendship is found in the mutual devotion and care shown by both parties. The more mutual the giving, the more balanced and solid the bond.

Possessing a generous heart and attitude is a God-given gift. We must refuse to fear that if we give too much we will be left with nothing. Satan would have us believe the lie that generosity leads to impoverishment and unmet needs. But our needs must be met only in God's will. Then, and only then, are we capable of turning and truly and guilelessly giving to others.

One of the most painful experiences in life is to be rejected. Inevitably, nearly every human soul is acquainted with this heartache. To be denied someone's love is not only painful and disappointing, but also it breaks the chain of love. It is difficult for us to give love when we don't receive it in return. But we must never forget that we were created to love; that is the highest commandment and commission for any human being.

Loving and giving are complementary and are closely intertwined. God so *loved* the world that he *gave* us his only Son. A love-filled heart produces the gesture of giving.

One of the wisest and most biblical solutions for breaking free from the destructive cycle of rejection and its resulting pain of loneliness is to cry out to God for his healing touch and then demonstrate God's love to us by showing love to another person. Joy and freedom run deepest in the life of a person whose heart is flooded with generosity.

One of the saddest human scenarios we can ever witness is the death of a person who has lived a life of loneliness and self-isolation. That person has left this earthly existence without having felt the warmth of someone's love or having invested his or her own tenderness and affection in another person's heart and soul. Regardless of what caused this sad condition, the result is always the same. That person has missed out on one of life's greatest joys and most rewarding experiences—genuine love.

We do not need more words. What we need is to touch God's heart and display it to others. God uses people to love and restore one another; he refuses to act alone. He delights in having his power and grace reproduced in his children. He desires to use us as an expression of his will.

Satan is determined to sabotage our communion with God and with one another. His desire is to destroy our relationships, to isolate us, and to systematically fill our minds with deception and our hearts with discouragement and despair. He is not ignorant of God's wisdom; he knows that God's people are strong and well-protected when they are united as an army.

When we look carefully at God's Word, we see

Teach Me to Be Generous

over and over again his desire: that we love one another. From the writings of John, Peter, Paul, and others, we find a profound influence of God's love, and an emphasis on how essential it is that we truly love one another. The commandment states clearly, "You shall love your neighbor as yourself" (Matt. 19:19).

Dear Lord,
I ask for a generous heart and a giving attitude.
Display your great grace in me by helping me to
reach out lovingly to others.

CHAPTER 19

TURN MY EYES

AWAY FROM

USELESS THINGS

*Turn away my eyes from looking at worthless
things, / And revive me in Your way.*

(Ps. 119:37)

Do not love the world or the things in the world.
If anyone loves the world, the love of the
Father is not in him.

(1 John 2:15)

A multitude of things seem to
compete daily for our atten-
tion. Sorting through the affairs of life and picking

out what is of value is one of life's greatest challenges. The most successful people in the world are those who have learned to concentrate on the most important matters, while sometimes putting some very good things aside. That isn't easy!

Time demands that only so much can be accomplished in any given day, and so we must make choices according to what is most important in our lives. A person without priorities is like a lost sailor at the mercy of the wind and the waves.

Sorting out what is the most appropriate in life often means that we must distinguish between what is good and what is best. And the good and the best are often competitors. If we want the best out of life, we have to determine ahead of time which things fall into that category and then put our time and energy toward them.

Once we have been touched by God, we begin to realize that the *best* in life is seeking his kingdom and doing his will. We can be sure that doing God's will is never a passive matter. It's erroneous to think that when we are truly committed to God we will sit around waiting for directives. His initial directions will give us so much to do that we will never become bored. We must avoid saying, "I can't move until God moves me." When we have no clear direction in life, we must *move toward God*. If we apply all our energy to seeking him, we can enjoy the excitement of all that we are learning and experiencing.

If we truly belong to Christ, we can expect that there will be times when he motions for our attention so that he can show us how to adjust our priorities. Then there are times when God doesn't require us to evaluate our lives by close examination. Instead, he simply allows an earthquake to rearrange our lives. When everything that can be shaken is shaken, we eventually rummage through the debris to determine what is still valuable to us, and more so to him.

The only reason why God allows difficult times such as these is that great gain will eventually come after unimportant things are swept out of the way. We must never assume that God delights in some kind of harsh testing program for his children that he designed in order to see just how much we can take. Everything that comes from God's hand to his children, whether it appears difficult or easy, always comes from a Father's heart that desires to mature and bless us.

God wants to bridge the distance between our

heads and our hearts. He delights in a committed heart—never an outward "form of godliness."

In order to keep our life priorities as uncomplicated as possible, we must evolve from "head faith" to "heart faith." We cannot merely acknowledge God with our minds, we must also consecrate our whole hearts to him and learn to want what he wants. We sometimes try to walk with God while saving our hearts for the things this world readily offers. But such a walk leaves our souls fragmented and our lives unfulfilled. We forget the simple truth in Matthew 6:21: "For where your treasure is, there your heart will be also."

A consecrated love for God requires no less than everything. However, God is not a stingy, legalistic Father who wants his children to be deprived or neglected. "Every good gift and every perfect gift is from above, and comes down from the Father of lights, with whom there is no variation or shadow of turning" (James 1:17).

God looks on the heart. The habits of our hearts reveal how real our faith is in him. Regardless of how well our hearts are doing, there is still a "mixture" in the human soul and spirit to be dealt with; pollution has slowly and quietly seeped into us from the world, the flesh, and the devil. Often this mixture goes unnoticed or even ignored by God's people.

What remains when our personal world is violently shaken and tested by circumstances? What or who is left to believe in? What is important to us, and why? Difficult times often uncover hidden and dormant "heart sets" that are not revealed during times of abundance and prosperity. What are our priorities once the luxuries of life disappear and our absolute helplessness is exposed? This exposure can be shocking and painful, but ultimately it can bring us back to our knees, seeking God's wonderful presence. It can return us once again to the basics of our faith. God must be God, and he must reside at the center of all we do, all we are, and all we ever hope to be.

We need to ask God to cleanse us, repair us, and give us new hearts. The process requires that we surrender to him, pray diligently, and wait patiently. If we do these things, we *can* learn to turn away from useless things and cherish all that God cherishes.

Dear Lord,
Should I forget, as I often do, please remind me

how transitory this world really is. Help me to keep in mind that it will all soon pass away and that all that will be left is my relationship with you.

CHAPTER 20

FORGIVE

MY MANY SINS

Have mercy upon me, O God, / According to Your lovingkindness; / According to the multitude of Your tender mercies, / *Blot out my transgressions. / Wash me thoroughly from my iniquity, / And cleanse me from my sin. . . . / Behold, I was brought forth in iniquity, / And in sin my mother conceived me. . . . / Purge me with hyssop, and I shall be clean; / Wash me, and I shall be whiter than snow.*

(Ps. 51:1–2, 5, 7)

"Come now, and let us reason together," / Says the LORD, / *"Though your sins are like scarlet, / They shall be as white as snow."*

(Isa. 1:18)

*I*mperfections in an object are often not obvious until the object is placed beside a similar object that is unblemished. We seldom appreciate the true quality of an item until we compare it to its original design. In a similar way, our personal inherent flaws and lack of virtues are brought into clearer focus when we are face to face with the Person who designed us in his own image.

If at this very moment we were to enter directly into the presence of God, we would instantly realize how different we are from our Creator and from what we should be. Recognizing this difference, the children of Israel feared for their lives in the presence of God. They said to Moses, "You speak with us, and we will hear; but let not God speak with us, lest we die" (Ex. 20:19).

Few people would argue that our basic fallen nature could compare or compete with that of our Creator. It is sad that in our present world God's righteous qualities are rarely seen or displayed in his creation. As our world continually attempts to solve its problems apart from God, the expanse between good and evil widens, and the contrast between purity and pollution is gravely apparent.

When we become profoundly aware of the depravity and sin in our society and of the wickedness in our own character, our hearts may sink in despair and our souls feel desolate and empty. Truly, we cannot live lives of sin before God's presence.

But we can be thankful that we do have an Advocate. He is God's atonement for our sins—One who is willing to stand in our place and plead on our behalf. His name is Jesus, and he paved the way for all humankind to be forgiven and redeemed, so that we could have eternal life. By his grace we can enjoy fellowship with God now and for eternity.

It is our unwillingness to surrender to God that precludes salvation. Jesus was not born into the world to condemn it, but to redeem it. He came that the world might know the love of the Father and be saved.

Father God rules the world first by his love and then by his power. If power were his main emphasis, we would all find ourselves prostrate and overcome before him. But our God knows our fragile frame and our natural inclination to sin. Our humanity does not diminish his divinity or extinguish his love.

Sadly, God finds it difficult to develop a love relationship with some of his children, because they find living in the light of his love and his power uncomfortable. God's light exposes all that resides in the human soul. That light discloses the hidden secrets of the heart. This exposure causes many of us to run from God into the arms of self-justification, denial, and deception. We would be wise to recognize that we are all naked before God's holy eyes. With that knowledge we need to consider and take account of what kinds of unholiness reside in our hearts.

Sin is deadly from every perspective. We can't hide our sinfulness any more than we can hide one of the oceans. And we can't ignore it anymore than we can ignore poison once it has entered our stomachs. Yet God's love is unconditionally available to us. He wants to help us.

Our tendency toward sin does not surprise God, but the unnecessary pain and destruction it produces grieves his heart. God's desire is not to condemn or damn his own creation but to apprehend our hearts and souls, bring us to an awareness of our wrongdoings, and then restore us and give us new life.

The forgiveness and cleansing we so desperately need come only through Jesus. There is no other way to deal with sin and its ultimate judgment than for someone else to pay the price as our substitute so that we can go free. Christ is that person. Our wrongs in life will not arbitrarily be forgotten. There is a payment to be paid for sin. God has already made this payment through Christ, but his payment is valid only if we accept it. Nothing but his blood, as a payment for ours, will take away sin. John taught that if we confess our sins, God is faithful and just and will forgive us for our sins and cleanse us from all unrighteousness (1 John 1:9).

The incomprehensible is ours to comprehend. The price has been paid for us to enter into God's holy presence now and for all eternity. Jesus opened that door. And we have an open invitation to receive and take hold of total forgiveness for all our sins, and of hope for our futures.

What a marvelous God we have—One who is willing to do so much for us if we will only ask.

Dearest Father God,
Thank you for the gift of your Son, Jesus, and for
the forgiveness and cleansing that come through
him. Let no sin, either known or unknown, reside
in me, but rather work in me a purified life.